Korin
from
Charles

This book applies some of the procedures of modern critical theory (in particular reception-theory, deconstruction, theories of dialogue and the hermeneutics associated with the German philosopher Gadamer) to the interpretation of Latin poetry. Charles Martindale argues, against the positivistic and historicist approaches still dominant within Latin studies, that we neither can nor should attempt to return to an 'original' meaning for ancient poems free from later accretions and the processes of appropriation; more traditional approaches to literary enquiry conceal a metaphysics (of the text-in-itself) which has been put in question by various anti-foundationalist accounts of the nature of meaning and the relationship between language and what it describes. From this perspective the author examines different readings of the poetry of Virgil, Ovid, Horace and Lucan, in order to suggest alternative ways in which those texts might more profitably be read. Finally he focuses on a key term for such study: 'translation', and examines the epistemological questions it raises and seeks to circumvent. He thus proposes a revised programme for the study of what we term 'antiquity', and a 'postmodern' poetics.

ROMAN LITERATURE
AND ITS CONTEXTS

Redeeming the text

ROMAN LITERATURE
AND ITS CONTEXTS

Series editors:
Denis Feeney and Stephen Hinds

The editors of this series share the growing belief that the dominant modes of study of Roman literature are insufficiently in touch with current research in other areas of the classics, and in the humanities at large. Students of Greek literature, in the best traditions of classical scholarship, have been strengthening their contacts with cognate fields such as social history, anthropology, history of thought, linguistics and literary theory; the study of Roman literature has just as much to gain from engaging with these other contexts and intellectual traditions. The series is designed to encourage readers of Latin texts to sharpen their readings by placing them in broader and better-defined contexts, and to encourage other classicists to explore the general or particular implications of their work for readers of Latin texts. The books all constitute original and innovative research and are envisaged as suggestive essays whose aim is to stimulate debate.

Other books in the series:

Philip Hardie, *The epic successors of Virgil: a study in the dynamics of a tradition*

Duncan F. Kennedy, *The arts of love: five studies in the discourse of Roman love elegy*

Redeeming the text

Latin poetry and the hermeneutics of reception

Charles Martindale

Professor of Latin,
University of Bristol

Published by the Press Syndicate of the University of Cambridge
The Pitt Building, Trumpington Street, Cambridge CB2 1RP
40 West 20th Street, New York NY 10011-4211, USA
10 Stamford Road, Oakleigh, Victoria 3166, Australia

First published 1993

Printed in Great Britain at the University Press, Cambridge

A catalogue record for this book is available from the British Library

Library of Congress cataloguing in publication data
Martindale, Charles.
Redeeming the text: Latin poetry and the heremeneutics of reception /
by Charles Martindale.
p.   cm. – (Roman literature and its contexts)
Includes bibliographical references and index.
ISBN 0 521 41717 1 (hc). – ISBN 0 521 42719 3 (pb)
1. Latin poetry – History and criticism – Theory etc.
2. Reader-response criticism.   3. Hermeneutics.   I. Title.   II. Series.
PA6047.M28   1993
871'.0109 – dc20   92–4116   CIP

ISBN 0 521 41717 1 hardback
ISBN 0 521 42719 3 paperback

This book
is
dedicated
to
D.F.K.
for minding, for arguing,
and
(above all)
for making me laugh.

Redeeming time when men think least I will.

Prince Hal, *Henry IV pt I*

Redeem the time, redeem the dream

. . .

And after this our exile.

T.S. Eliot

Contents

CONTENTS

Plates

(between pages 60 and 61)

1 Claude Lorrain, *The Landing of Aeneas in Latium*, 1675. Oil on canvas, 1.75 × 2.25 m. Anglesey Abbey, National Trust (Lord Fairhaven Collection). *Photo*: NTPL/John Bethell

2 Titian, *Diana and Actaeon*, 1556–9. Canvas, 1.88 × 2.06 m. Edinburgh, Duke of Sutherland Collection, on loan to the National Gallery of Scotland. *Photo*: National Galleries of Scotland

3 Titian, *The Death of Actaeon*, 1570–5. Canvas, 1.79 × 1.98 m. London, National Gallery. *Photo*: National Gallery.

4 Titian, *The Flaying of Marsyas*, 1570–5. Canvas, 213 × 2.075 m. Kremsier, Archiepiscopal Palace. *Photo*: Prudence Cuming Associates Ltd

Preface

The aim of this *libellus* is to outline an alternative approach to the positivistic modes of interpretation (with their teleological assumptions) still dominant in Latin studies, which reflect the certainties and settled procedures of the 'Enlightenment' – trust in measuring and observation, commitment to a single rational method, belief in progress, and so forth – certainties and procedures which, during this century, have come under pressure from various sources, including new scientific and philosophical models. I shall in particular argue that the interpretation of texts is inseparable from the history of their reception. It follows that the classical world cannot be coherently studied in isolation, if we are to try to articulate the history and status of our current goals and assumptions. Accordingly I attempt to make a case for a broadly-conceived, dialectical classics, rescued from its current partial ghettoization.

Much of my previous published work has taken the form of investigations into the influence of Latin on English poetry. I would like now to put this mainly practical enquiry onto a firmer theoretical footing. The reader will notice a number of principal strands in my current thinking, in addition to the traces (and more) of the traditional classics within which I was initially educated: the New Criticism, with its commitment to close textual reading which still seems to me invaluable; deconstruction, in its Derridean guise; theories of dialogue, in particular those of Bakhtin and Gadamer; reception theory. At times my argument will take a metaphysical turn; several of the problems discussed by modern theorists are also at issue, if in a different form, in classical theology. The widespread refusal to take metaphysical questions seriously has, unsurprisingly, led to much bad (and occluded) metaphysics, in literary analysis as well as elsewhere. It is thus appropriate that T.S.

Eliot's is a name which will recur; his great meditative sequence *Four Quartets* is, to my thinking, among the profoundest treatments of time and place and history and memory we have. Despite recent attempts to dismiss or ignore him, he remains one of the most influential figures of our century, one whom, far from having outstripped, we have yet to catch up with.

In escaping one parochial orthodoxy we should not merely exchange it for another, for example some putative 'New Classics' built on a narrow base of 'theory' alone. Among thinkers revered by the 'theorists' are a number whose work has important implications for the study of literature, but there are innumerable other writers, both of this and of previous centuries, of whom this is also the case. As individuals we cannot study them all. As a profession we should not confine ourselves to narrow canons constructed by authoritarians old or new.

The structure of the book is more cumulative than sequential. In the first chapter I set out some of the main areas of concern, paradigms and concepts (in particular issues of reception, context, history, tradition and dialogue), to which I then keep returning, in subsequent chapters, probing them from slightly different angles and within differing theoretical models, and exploring their implication for the interpretation of particular writers and particular poems. Each chapter is also designed to be readable as a separate essay; readers whose taste for exegesis of texts exceeds their interest in explicit matters of theory may prefer to begin with one of the later chapters. My overall aim is less to present a single coherent theory of reading than to explore the implications of certain emphases and modes of procedure within literary enquiry as currently constituted. It is indeed one of the book's theses that there are virtues in recognizing the provisionality of even those procedures to which we are most committed; in the end (indeed at the beginning) we have no choice but to interpret, and the good critic will not flinch from making a virtue of necessity, but not before recognizing the right of other accounts to make themselves heard.

Appropriately a book arguing for the merits of dialogue is itself the locus of many dialogues. I owe a great deal to my three editors, Pauline Hire of Cambridge University Press, Denis Feeney and Stephen Hinds, for encouragement, help and constructive criticism, and for occasionally saving me from myself. I have been singularly fortunate in my colleagues, first at Sussex and then at Bristol. At Sussex, a university committed to interdisciplinary study, I learned from colleagues in many subject areas:

not least from Bernard Harrison, Gabriel Josipovici, Larry Lerner, Stephen Medcalf, Tony Nuttall and Alan Sinfield. At Bristol I have benefited from a number of sites for dialogue: in particular the Classical Departmental Seminar, which explores new intellectual developments in the classical area; the English–Latin Seminar, run jointly between the two departments for both staff and students, at which we have explored many of the issues and poems discussed here; and a third-year special option, 'The Classical Heritage', which I taught to a group of students in the 1990/91 session; and here I must mention, in particular, the contributions of Isabelle Burbidge, Fiona Cox, Julia Paulman, Shelley Sanders, Elizabeth Wells. Among colleagues at Bristol I have never failed to learn from dialogue with Tom Mason and George Myerson, from the English Department, with Michael Liversidge from the Art History Department, or with John Gould and Christopher Rowe (whose measured scepticism has had more influence on me than he probably realizes) from my own. I must also thank: other Bristol students, Julia Hoffbrand, Julian Holmes, Alex Langdon, Sarah Loom, Philip Young; colleagues from outside Bristol, Colin Burrow, Don Fowler, Philip Hardie (the author of another book in this series which he kindly let me read in draft), Robert Parker; members of my family, Gabriel Martindale (my youngest interlocutor), Michelle Martindale (who pointed me towards a number of instructive passages and displayed, as ever, finesse in close reading), Joanna Parker. Finally four people, who are both colleagues and friends, must receive separate mention. Terry McKiernan taught me the pleasures (and pains) of merely circulating, with a tact and subtlety of which only he is capable, as well as not letting me get away with all my outrageous assertions. Catharine Edwards (although she may not believe it) has influenced me in multifarious ways, not least in bringing me to a less narrow conception of history and of issues in feminism. David Hopkins has argued with (and not infrequently against) me about literature and life with a persistence and integrity reminiscent of Dr Johnson, his favourite critic, and tried to keep me, I fear in vain, from wandering too far from the Path of Truth. Finally there is the dedicatee Duncan Kennedy, without whom this book would certainly never have been written. He may take this as a doubtful compliment, and will, I expect, dissent from much that I have to say (and even where he might have wished to claim authorship, he will probably feel I have spoiled those ideas of his which I have appropriated and recontextualized). Perhaps, when he reads the results, he may think that all those hours of patient (if at times hilarious) conversation could have been more profitably employed. But I hope that he will agree that, in intellectual matters, as in life generally, it is usually better to travel hopefully than to arrive. The issue of the addressee (or 'implied reader') of these words I leave on one side, although it is one which will re-emerge, obliquely, from time to time, in what follows.

Texts and translations, except where specified, are my own. In accordance with the style of the series, documentation has been kept to a minimum. Apologies are due for any unacknowledged (or unrecognized) intertextualities.

C.A.M.
Shoreham-by-Sea
and Bristol
October 1991

Acknowledgements

I presented some of the ideas explored in this book, in rather more polemical fashion, in an essay entitled 'Redeeming the text: the validity of comparisons of Classical and post-Classical literature', published in *Arion*. In chapter 4 I rework some material from 'Unlocking the word-hoard: in praise of metaphrase', in E. Shaffer (ed.), *Comparative Literature* 6, 47–72, published by Cambridge University Press. I am grateful for permission to reuse this earlier material.

Thanks are due to the following for their permission to reproduce copyright material: To Faber & Faber Ltd and Harcourt Brace Jovanovich for excerpts from 'Ash Wednesday' from *Collected Poems 1909–1962* by T.S. Eliot, copyright by Harcourt Brace Jovanovich, Inc.; copyright 1963, 1964 by T.S. Eliot; from 'The Four Quartets' from *Collected Poems 1909–1962* by T.S. Eliot, copyright by Harcourt Brace Jovanovich, Inc.; copyright 1963, 1964 by T.S. Eliot; and from 'The Waste Land' from *Collected Poems 1909–1962* by T.S. Eliot, copyright 1936 by Hartcourt Brace Jovanovich, Inc.; copyright 1963, 1964 by T.S. Eliot. To Faber & Faber Ltd and Alfred A. Knopf, Inc. for the excerpt from *Collected Poems* by Wallace Stevens, copyright 1942 by Wallace Stevens and renewed 1970 by Holly Stevens. To Chatto & Windus Ltd and Grove Press, Inc. for the excerpt from *The Last World* by Christian Ransmayr, translated by John Woods, copyright 1990. To Victor Gollancz Ltd, and Donald C. Farber and Dell Publishing Co. for the excerpt from *Cat's Cradle* by Kurt Vonnegut, copyright 1963. To Frederick Warne & Co. for the excerpt from *The Tale of Timmy Tiptoes* by Beatrix Potter, copyright 1911.

I

Five concepts in search of an author: suite

Whether you can observe a thing or not depends on the theory which you use. It is the theory which decides what can be observed.

Einstein to Heisenberg

'Lor!', cried Mrs. Boffin. 'What I say is, the world's wide enough for all of us!'

'So it is, my dear', said Mr. Boffin, 'when not literary. But when so, not so.'

. . .

'But what was tokenz?'

'Marks', said Mr. Podsnap; 'Signs, you know, Appearances – Traces.'

'Ah! Of a Orse?' inquired the foreign gentleman.

Our Mutual Friend

The first little bird flew into the bush . . . , and it sang – 'Who's bin digging-up *my* nuts? Who's been digging-up *my*-nuts?'

Timmy Tiptoes went on with his work without replying; indeed the little bird did not expect an answer. It was only singing its natural song, and it meant nothing at all. But when the other squirrels heard that song they rushed upon Timmy Tiptoes and cuffed and scratched him, and upset his bag of nuts.

The Tale of Timmy Tiptoes

> Words strain,
> Crack and sometimes break, under the burden,
> Under the tension, slip, slide, perish,
> Decay with imprecision, will not stay in place,
> Will not stay still.

T.S. Eliot

'The question is', said Alice, 'whether you *can* make words mean so many different things.'

'The question is', said Humpty Dumpty, 'which is to be master – that's all.'

Through the Looking Glass

1 Two short (tall?) stories

I offer two short stories about the world we inhabit and how we can know it. According to the first story we can survey the world, disinterestedly, 'from outside' and, at least to some degree, arrive at a rational (God's-eye) view of its constitution. According to the second story, the character of our knowledge is always dependent on the observer's angle of vision, and phenomena are only describable from 'within' particular discourses,[1] which indeed determine what are to count as 'the phenomena' in the first place. We can call the first story the Newtonian story, the story of 'Enlightenment' (a story which has brought us much that we, in the West, hold most dear, over a large range of human activities). The second story we can call the Einsteinian story,[2] the story of 'Modernism'. This book could be described as an attempt to think through some of the implications of inhabiting this second story for the study of what we call 'ancient' literature.

2 Are you receiving me?

There are many versions of 'reception theory', but, on any of them, interpretation cannot be separated from the ways texts are, and have been, received by readers. Let a poet start the conversation:

> I met a traveller from an antique land
> Who said: 'Two vast and trunkless legs of stone
> Stand in the desert. Near them, on the sand,
> Half-sunk a shattered visage lies, whose frown,
> And wrinkled lip, and sneer of cold command,

[1] Cf. Veyne (1988a), who uses the image of a fish-bowl (118).

[2] For the importance of Einstein, and especially his paper of 1905, 'The electrodynamics of moving bodies', for literary theory see Holquist (1990) especially 20–1, 156–62. A number of earlier writers can, of course, easily be appropriated for 'Modernism' (Montaigne, Sterne, etc.).

Tell that its sculptor well those passions read
Which yet survive, stamped on these lifeless things,
The hand that mocked them and the heart that fed;
And on the pedestal these words appear:
'My name is Ozymandias, king of kings –
Look on my works, ye mighty, and despair!'
Nothing beside remains. Round the decay
Of that colossal wreck, boundless and bare
The lone and level sands stretch far away.

We could interpret this poem as a fable about reception. How, for example, should the inscription be read? Is it a sign of Ozymandias' authority? Or rather of the transience of all earthly power? The poem embodies a clash of viewpoints, and, consequent on this, a clash of readings. In the presumed historical context we have both Ozymandias' view and the view of the artist who mocked the king's pretensions and yet produced a work of art (this on the assumption that, in the ambiguous eighth line 'the hand that mocked them and the heart that fed [i.e. 'them': 'the passions'], the hand and heart are, respectively, those of the artist and the king, and are the objects of 'survive', taken as a transitive verb). Each finds a different meaning in the statue. But there are at least two further possible viewpoints within the poem, the traveller's and that of 'I', the speaker of the lines who may, or may not, also be the poet Shelley. There could be a further implication that both art and human greatness survive, even amid an eternity of sand. Although tyrant and sculptor are now dead, Ozymandias' 'passions' outlast them both, and live on as depicted in the shattered fragments, and that despite the sculptor's placing mockery; yet they are also ironized by their new context. And the 'despair' which an onlooker now feels is presumably quite different from that envisaged by Ozymandias, monarch of all he surveyed. And the complexities do not stop there. For there is also the question of where authority resides, in the poem, for identifying, and describing, these diverse receptions. How reliable, in other words, are the various voices and the claims made for them? And, beyond that, my reading of the poem, in the light of reception theory, becomes itself a tiny part of the dialogical processes of its reception and thus of any argument about its meaning. *Meaning*, could we say, *is always realized at the point of reception*; if so, we cannot assume that an 'intention' is effectively communicated within any text. And also, it appears, a writer *can never control the reception of his or her work*, with respect either to the character of the readership or to any use which is made of that work.

Let us juxtapose with the voice of 'Shelley' a second, more academic voice. In the *Journal of Roman Studies* for 1989 there appeared an essay on the *Eclogues* by Richard Jenkyns, which begins thus:

> There is an obstacle to our natural appreciation of Virgil's *Eclogues* which looms as large in their case as in that of any poetry whatever. . . . though they themselves take Theocritus as a model, they were to become the fountainhead from which the vast and diverse tradition of pastoral . . . was to spring. To use them as a model was in itself to distort their character . . . Moreover, the growth of the later pastoral tradition meant that many things were attributed to Virgil which are not in Virgil . . . It is hard, therefore, to approach the *Eclogues* openly and without preconceptions about what they contain . . . No poems perhaps have become so encrusted by the barnacles of later tradition and interpretation as these, and we need to scrape these away if we are to see them in their true shape.[3]

Anyone at all familiar with the writings of classical scholars will have met this kind of rhetoric before, for here we approach what is still, for many classicists, the holy of holies, the reified text-in-itself, its meaning placed beyond contingency. Produced in an apocalyptic moment of creation (like the emergence of Athena out of the head of Zeus) the text comes forth, fully armed with the intentions of its creator, and available and present to at least the wiser readers of the day. Unfortunately, during the intervening years, it suffers depredations from the follies, incompetences and sheer ignorance and naivety of our nearer ancestors (particularly those unfortunate enough to live in the Middle Ages, as we quaintly call the thousand years from St Augustine to Dante). Luckily modern classical philology is at hand, to roll back the years and reveal to us the original in all its gleaming, pristine purity. I exaggerate, of course, but not much (and will my irony help, or hinder, the reception I hope for, but cannot control?).

Some of the terms Jenkyns uses to valorize his approach merit further inspection. For example, he starts by invoking the discourse of the 'natural'; a competent reader, it is implied, would, 'naturally' and

---

[3] Jenkyns (1989), 26. Further quotations (in order) are from 26, 29, 35, 31, 37, 36. When Jenkyns invokes such parallels as *Le Grand Meaulnes*, we see the discourse deconstructing itself (29). For the sensibility cf. Jenkyns (1980).

without excessive difficulty, arrive at an original meaning corresponding with the 'true shape' of the poems, were it not for the barriers interposed between reader and text by history, tradition and critical misinterpretation. But, it can be replied, this drive for interpretative singleness, far from being in any sense 'natural', has a history and is rooted in specific cultural practices; it would, for example, have surprised Dante, for whom the text was, precisely, 'polysemous', containing many signs, including allegorical senses not necessarily under the full control of the (human) author (*Letter to Can Grande*, 7). Jenkyns likewise draws a sharp distinction between what is '*in* Virgil' and interpretations 'put *upon* Virgil'; but such a distinction will only hold absolutely firm if we posit a 'metaphysics' of the text and a meaning immanent within the signs regardless of any readerly activity. Jenkyns urges us to approach the *Eclogues* 'without preconceptions' (while at the same time reminding us that they are modelled on Theocritus, and assigning them to the pastoral genre, thereby inviting a certain sort of reading); but any notion of a naked encounter between a text and a reader who is a sort of *tabula rasa* is absurd. We all approach the reading of texts with the baggage of our values and our experience, with certain categories, assumptions, prejudices and 'fore-understandings'. To have such baggage is what it is to be a human being in history; *without it we could not read at all*. It is easy to show how Jenkyns' own essay can readily be situated in a particular time and particular place, dependent on particular (contestable) methods of interpretation, and revealing particular (equally contestable) local tastes, containing the traces of the Victorian writers Jenkyns so admires, and with ideological implications which could be further unpacked. Thus Jenkyns, we may note, finds 'a sort of shy urgency' in 'the tiny scene of the children in the orchard' (8.37–41) which 'some have thought the most affecting thing in all the *Eclogues*' ('all is so small, all so tender'); of *Eclogue* 10 he writes 'one has only to read line 14 or line 52 aloud to hear their lovely cold romantic sounds'. Further instances of a post-Romantic sensibility of this kind include his remarks on 'the mystery of ocean or its perennity or even its salt indifference', or his references to the 'sweet, pretty' world of the Italians in the *Aeneid*, and the 'modest country-gentlemanliness' of Evander's life-style. None of this, of course, means that Jenkyns' reading is a purely subjective or private one. Rather it reflects public argument, and institutional practices and questions. It is enmeshed in previous readings by previous reading communities, and thus testifies to much wider agreements and disagreements than the merely here and now. Or rather the here and now is always the locus of discourses stretching back into a largely lost past and forwards to an unknown future. But, for all that, it is evidently the view of a British scholar of 'our' time.

'Jenkyns', we may say, is enlisting, in support of his own reading, the authority of a particular (here mystified) version of historicist discourse. In Classics one of the founding documents of this brand of historicism is Wolf's *Prolegomena ad Homerum* of 1795. In a letter to Heyne, Wolf stated that 'the most pernicious' of the obstacles to 'genuinely historical research' are the opinions 'which attempt to adapt antiquity to our taste, our scholarly desires and artistic ideas'.[4] In practice, however, readers may find their responses modified by a reading of 'Homer'. Thus, just as the use of 'our' smooths away competing tastes, so too such a notion of the formation of taste seems to ignore the influence of the past on the present. We do not merely interpret 'Homer' by the light of our taste, since the Homeric poems have themselves contributed to the formation of that taste. Historicism of this kind in the end denies history. Homer has been changed for us by Virgil and Milton, who have left their traces in his text, and thereby enabled new possibilities of meaning. Aesthetic preferences and supposedly 'pure' historical judgements in the event prove inseparable, as Wolf's own judgements can illustrate. Indeed we need to remember the historical contingency of the categories involved, categories including 'the aesthetic' and 'the historical'.

Two views about the significance of works of art are not infrequently set in opposition. The first ('humanistic') view is that such works are the vehicles of eternally valid truths and experiences (but it may be doubted whether such verities exist or, if they did, whether we could recognize them). The second is that these works are wholly or largely contingent on an original set of historical determinants (but against this clearly readers can both enjoy, and advance persuasive readings of, works about whose historical circumstances they know little, or nothing). Again a widespread recognition that, almost inevitably, we read *from the present interest* conflicts with a desire for otherness and a supposed recognition, or experience, of it during the process of reading; theorizing the gap has, however, proved difficult.[5] In this book, in an attempt to negotiate these two sets of conflicting positions, I shall explore a historicized version of

---

[4] Wolf (1985), 246.

[5] Thus in Beer (1989), 1 there is a lack of 'middle' between the claims in the first and second paragraphs ('Literary history . . . starts now . . . Engaging with the *difference* of the past . . .).

reception theory, associated above all with Hans Robert Jauss; but it will be one of a less positivisitic character, which will concede rather more than he does to the operations of *différance*, the key term of Derrida's, which combines the idea of difference (meaning is an effect of the contrast between signs) and deferral (meaning always resists closure, a final – or originary – meaning, because signs never stand still). Jauss's 'reception-aesthetic' (to use his preferred designation) is linked with the German hermeneutical tradition culminating in Hans-Georg Gadamer's important work *Truth and Method*, published in 1960 (the 'and' of the title is disjunctive). On Gadamer's view 'the truth of works of art is a contingent one: what they reveal is dependent on the lives, circumstances and views of the audience to whom they reveal it'.[6] In Gadamer's words, 'It is part of the historical finiteness of our being that we are aware that after us others will understand in a different way'. Understanding in which 'the dead trace of meaning' is 'transformed back into living experience'[7] is always made *within history*; indeed our historicity is a necessary concomitant of understanding of this kind. Beliefs and fore-understandings ('prejudices' to use Gadamer's word) are not barriers to understanding but their precondition.[8] Interpretation also involves a constantly moving 'fusion of horizons' between past and present, text and interpreter. Accordingly, to use a more Eliotic formulation, we have to learn to respect not only the presentness of the present but also its pastness, and not only the pastness of the past but also its presentness.

From such a reception-theory stance I shall advance two theses, one 'weak' and the other 'strong'. The weak thesis is that numerous unexplored insights into ancient literature are locked up in imitations, translations and so forth (this thesis may be uncontroversial, but it is more honoured in the breach than the observance). The 'strong' thesis is that our current interpretations of ancient texts, whether or not we are aware of it, are, in complex ways, constructed by the chain of receptions through which their continued readability has been effected. As a result we cannot get back to any originary meaning wholly free of subsequent accretions. Meaning is produced and exchanged socially and discursively, and this is true of reading, even in a society like ours, in which it has become, to a greater or lesser degree, a 'private' activity. In order to be read, a text has to be made *readable*, in a complex process which begins

[6] Warnke (1987), 66.   [7] Gadamer (1975), 336, 146.
[8] Cf. Michaels (1978), 780: 'Meaning is not filtered through what we believe, it is constituted by what we believe'; cf. 782, and Gadamer (1975), 358.

with the acculturation of children and continues through educational institutions to wider interpretative groups. If we take the case of Homer and Virgil, the weak thesis would be that Virgil gives us powerful insights into Homer; the strong thesis, that, since Virgil, no reading of Homer, at least in the West, has been, *or could be*, wholly free of a vestigial Virgilian presence – not even one given by an interpreter not directly familiar with Virgil's poems – because the Homer–Virgil opposition is so deeply inscribed, both in the exegetical tradition and in the wider culture, because the two texts are always and already culturally implicated. In general poets have played the largest part in creating our sense of what earlier poems can 'mean', partly because their 'readings' have carried such cultural authority.

Accordingly, when we read an ancient poem, we have to remember the vast amount of cultural activity over the centuries which has made it possible for us to do so, including such material and institutional factors as scriptoria, publishing houses and the whole apparatus of scholarship, together with countless acts of appropriation by readers. To take a specific instance: 'Horace' and 'Horatian' are ideological signifiers, always already written but always on the move. Tennyson's 'To the Rev. F.D. Maurice', for example, can be read as an imitation, or recreation, of the Horatian invitation poem, its stanzas recalling Horace's Alcaics and echoing one of Horace's most famous phrases ('far from noise and smoke of town' recalls *C.* 3.29.12). The young Tennyson, we are told, had learned the Odes by heart, and thoroughly internalized what they stood for. Tennyson is writing to a friend who was a classical scholar and a unitarian minister, and who had aroused hostility by denying the doctrine of Hell. Tennyson, a modern 'Horace', invites him to the Isle of Wight to see his godson and to share conversation and companionship. Friendship thus blurs into Roman *amicitia* (indeed it is my contention that they cannot now be wholly disentangled), British imperial rule and the *pax Britannica* into the *imperium Romanum*, Christianity into pagan ethics, Tennyson in his house and garden into Horace on his Sabine estate. The poem is a small part of what 'Horace' now 'means'. And yet many scholars continue to believe that Horace is the 'same' today as he was 2,000 years ago.[9]

The point can perhaps be clarified by means of an example from one of literature's 'sister arts'. A form of historicism has now been operative for some time in the performance of 'early music'. Such 'authenticity', it is

---

[9] Cf. Smith (1988), 48, 53.

claimed, takes the listener back to a more accurate recreation of the original work in its first context. But, even if such a recreation were possible (anyway doubtful), how could we know, exactly, how such music was, 'then', 'received'? Richard Taruskin has argued, plausibly, that, behind the historicist crust, the crucial point about such performances, at their best, is rather their *modernity* (even if the appeal to the authority of a historicist discourse initially helped to validate the new approach). He shows how the style of performance can be linked with the aesthetics of Modernism, as defined by Pound and Eliot in literature, or by Stravinsky in music. Bach's 'authentic' interpreters are really 'reinterpreting' him 'for their own time – that is, for our time – the way all deathless texts must be reinterpreted if they are . . . to remain deathless'.[10] In a contribution to the ensuing debate, Charles Rosen, arguing that 'the philosophy of Early Music is indefensible, above all in its abstraction of original sound from everything which gave it meaning', concludes: 'Every performance today is a translation; a reconstruction of the original sound is the most misleading translation because it pretends to be the original, while the significance of the old sounds have irrevocably changed'.[11] The musical analogy can also assist in destabilizing reified conceptions of the literary text. We can readily concede that a musical performance, though necessarily time-bound, can be a wholly satisfactory 'realization' of a score on a particular occasion, without thereby becoming in any sense definitive. Moreover we have been shown that a work like Handel's *Messiah* was performed by the composer in different versions on different occasions, and was only given a single canonical form by subsequent editors and performers. With music the metaphysical 'text-in-itself' is more evidently a mirage.

Jauss's historicized version of reception theory is not without its defects. It exaggerates the knowledge which we can have of earlier readers, thereby reverting to a positivism which it supposedly rejects. It over-emphasizes the conformity of reading practices within designated 'periods'. Indeed, on the model of reading I am proposing, the identity of a period is intricately connected with the cultural politics of reading; *a period is recognized as such only at the point of reception.* Confident divisions of period, whether ancient or modern, constitute an essentializing move. What we call 'our' time is always something made up of fragments of 'the past'. Similarly the boundaries we select for historical

[10] Taruskin (1988), 197.

[11] Rosen (1990), 52. I shall return to this argument in ch. 4; Rosen's formulation of it involves obvious reification ('the significance of the old sounds').

definition are always, from some other perspectives, tendentious, or arbitrary, or hegemonic. We privilege a 'period', or a 'culture', which we then define, and characterize, on the basis of our selection, eliding innumerable possible differences of place, life-style and discourse. Periodization – like the division into Antiquity and the Middle Ages, or Republic and Empire – is so engrained that we take it for granted (we can call this 'the ideology of periodization'). Similarly, since the 'present' is not one thing, the difference between past and present need not be seen as *necessarily* greater than the difference which exists today within a single 'culture'; thus 'understanding' some Romans may not be more difficult than understanding some of our fellow citizens.

In an anxiety to avoid the charge that reception theory treats all interpretations as equally valid, Jauss resorts to a variant of the traditional appeal to the 'verdict of the ages', redefined by him as 'the successive unfolding of the potential for meaning that is embedded in a work and actualized in the stages of its historical reception as it discloses itself to understanding judgement, so long as this faculty achieves in a controlled fashion the "fusion of horizons" in the encounter with tradition'.[12] Quite apart from the problem of deciding what constitutes an 'understanding' judgement (and who is to decide), the notion of 'potentiality' (i.e. that the various interpretations were, in a sense, always 'there') is either trivially true (the potential is whatever meaning has been assigned), or occluded idealism, or false. How, for example, could any Roman, before the rise of Christianity, have guessed that Ovid's *Metamorphoses* would be subjected to Christian allegorizations of a sophisticated and comprehensive kind (whereby, for example, the story of Orpheus became, *inter alia*, an allegory about Christ and the human soul), which may well have appeared to readers operating within new paradigms of interpretation reasonable, authoritative, or even inevitable? If interpretation is contingent, then its future is unknowable in advance. For Jauss, by contrast, reception is, in Aristotelian fashion, organically inevitable rather than historically contingent. In the next section I shall accordingly modify Jauss's picture in the light of other, more deconstructionist models of dissemination. But the central point, I believe, still holds. What else indeed could (say) 'Virgil' be other than what readers have made of him over the centuries?

[12] Jauss (1982), 30; cf. the idea of 'horizons of potentiality' in Booth (1988), 91, and cf. 86.

3 Framing contexts

We can look again at what to many is the 'scandal' of interpretation, the fact that texts can be read so variously, that meanings proliferate. This proliferation is not, however, a purely arbitrary process, for there is always a connection between the framework within which we read texts and the interpretations we give of them (which is not to deny that our reading practices may themselves be interrogated, and modified, during the reading process). The point can be illustrated by looking, briefly, at two competing readings of Horace *Odes* 1.20. The piece is usually read, against a discourse of patronage or *amicitia* (that network of mutual obligations which bound together Roman society), as a panegyric of Maecenas, recalling his recovery from illness. Horace invites his grand 'friend' to dine with him; while he cannot serve the expensive wines Maecenas is used to, he will provide a wine with sentimental value, bottled by his own hand, on the 'farm' Maecenas had himself given him. In line 5 (if *clare* rather than *care* is read) we may be reminded, obliquely and ingeniously, that Maecenas preferred to stay within his original status as an *eques* (*clarus* was normally applied to senators), despite his wealth and his influence with the *princeps*. The contrast between the (comparative) poverty of the poet–friend and the greatness and wealth of the addressee was, it is claimed, conventional in such poems, reflecting social values and a preoccupation with status. An alternative reading has been proposed by Colin Macleod, who sees the Ode, against an Epicurean grid, as concerned with the dangers of success, to which are opposed the philosophical ideals of friendship and privacy.[13] Macleod finds a significant contrast between the wine which has been stored for a long time (*conditum*) and the acclaim given once only in public at the theatre (*datus*), which he reads as an implied depreciation of public success. So too with the contrast of wines: Horace is free since expensive wines do not control his cups (let Maecenas take note). On what basis do we adjudicate between these two readings? And in this case, we may observe, they are, as well as being different, not readily commensurable readings, so that it is not easy to resort to the common tactic of suggesting that both are partial and proposing a third which incorporates the other two. Each interpretation has its own precision; each interprets what it sees as the significant data. Choice between them is likely to depend on

---

[13] Macleod (1983), 225–9; cf. Nisbet and Hubbard (1970), commentary *ad loc.*

our overall view of 'Horace' and the general character of his work. But that, in turn, rests on innumerable other interpretative acts, every one of them open to dispute or revision, and dependent on prior reading strategies. Words will not stay still.

New reading practices accordingly bring new readings, for example, those recently constituted within 'feminism'. The presentation of Cleopatra in *Odes* 1.37, and in particular the apparent about-turn in that presentation in the final stanzas, has been variously discussed and accounted for. Steele Commager's seductive New Critical reading, in terms of 'antithetical and metaphorical structures' creating 'a double moral commitment' within a 'tense unity', stresses the poem's 'denseness of verbal suggestion' by which 'history has been concentrated into image'.[14] This approach can be compared with contemporary readings of Donne or Shakespeare (to which Commager refers), or of Marvell's 'Horatian Ode' for Cromwell (a poem partly imitative of 1.37) which became, in the hands of Eliot and his followers, something of a *locus classicus* for the virtues of 'maturity', 'poise', and 'ambivalence', in its presentation of historical figures. Feminism can offer us an alternative way of accounting for the poem's 'obliquities'. The now-traditional title, the 'Cleopatra Ode', is misleading, since her name is suppressed, unspeakable. The Ode attempts to fix the meaning of Actium in the West in terms of social, racial and sexual ideologies. *Libertas* resides with the victory of Caesar. The omission of other leading participants foregrounds the opposition between woman and man, the queen of Egypt and Rome's leader, the latter an embodiment of *virtus* (the quality of being a *vir*). Cleopatra thus becomes the 'Other' in terms of both race and sex. After the battle she is given the 'male' characteristics of bravery, philosophical equanimity and regal stature. This partial regendering (*nec muliebriter*) is the more surprising because the doves figuring her in line 18 are called *mollis*; we can map this word onto an epic discourse (an analogous simile is used of Achilles' pursuit of Hector in *Iliad* 22.139f.), but we can also map it onto a moral/sexual discourse which condemns *mollitia*, effeminacy, as a root cause of the decline of Rome. Thus Caesar brings a measure of enlightenment to Cleopatra by defeating her, and in this way enables her to transgress her gender (thus becoming 'other' in yet another sense), but only by death. How can 'women' 'win', within this

---

[14] Commager (1962), 88–97; quotations from (in order) 88, 91, 94, 93, 95. Among feminist readings of Latin poetry I am particularly indebted to the writings of Maria Wyke, especially her notion of the elegiac mistress as *scripta puella*: Wyke (1987).

discourse? This reading seems to offer as precise and comprehensive an account of the poem as Commager's. The common complaint that feminist readings emphasize some details at the expense of others misses the mark, since this is something all interpretations do – *and must do*. And in general feminists do not occlude their *interestedness*.

Texts, it may be, are endlessly *redescribable*. And they are constantly being made rereadable in multifarious ways, and in that sense are always 'in production'. Let us imagine we find a text in an unknown language, which is therefore initially unreadable. Or would it be better to call it a 'pre-text', for, if a text were not *already* readable, how could we know that it was a text? Entertaining the hypothesis of its potential readability, we find someone to translate it for us. The translated text is already an interpretation (see chapter 4), since translation depends on prior reading practices. We are now in a position to map that text onto some sort of interpretative matrix (to a large extent this has already been done in the act of translating). Today that matrix will usually be a historical one. The text is now readable *in a certain way*, but our original axioms are not transcended, nor what we constitute as our 'final vocabulary'.[15] We are moreover part of what we are describing. Critics and scholars attempt to establish stable grounds for interpretation in a number of different ways, including authorial intention, historical context, ideology, genre, literary history, the nature of language and so on. The catch is that all these are as problematic as the 'text', dependent on other 'texts', and susceptible themselves to destabilization.

The difficulties with intentionalism are now widely familiar. How far do we 'intend' what we say? Are words wholly under our control? Can we have knowledge of another person's consciousness? Do signs offer direct access to reality? And one trouble with contexts is that there are too many of them. Contexts are not single, nor are they found 'lying about' as it were;[16] we have to construct them from other texts, which also have to be interpreted. (And by text I mean any vehicle of signification, so that in this extended sense a mosaic, or a marriage ceremony, is a 'text' as much as a book.) For example, Sallust's Sempronia (*Cat.* 25), one of the 'new women' with a more 'emancipated' life-style who supposedly appeared in the late Republic, is frequently cited as an analogue for the mistresses presented, in more stylized form, in Roman erotic poetry; and, of course, a woman with this name existed, whereas Lesbia or Cynthia could be an

[15] Rorty (1989), 73 for this phrase.   [16] So Felperin (1990), 126.

invented character. But our only access to Sempronia is through a piece of writing, within a particular discourse, by an aristocratic, male politician, so that she too is a 'written woman'; we have no way of knowing how she would have described herself, whether she had internalized a discursive role like that mapped out in Sallust, and, if so, whether in all social contexts, or only in some, since particular modes of description are often specific to particular discourses. In Derrida's notorious phrase, 'there is no outside-text' ('il n'y a pas d'hors-texte'). This does not mean that there are no non-linguistic entities, rather that all meaning is generated, and exchanged, within some signifying system or other.[17] There is no unmediated access to 'reality'. As with historical context, so with genre. Francis Cairns argues that only if we recover the precise ancient understanding of genre (as set out, for example, in Menander Rhetor, a Greek rhetorical writer of the third century AD) can we give a true account of ancient texts. In connection with the supposed continuity of ancient generic practices, he claims that 'in a very real sense antiquity was in comparison with the nineteenth and twentieth centuries a time-free zone'.[18] Thus, in his search for an objective, non-contingent basis for interpretation, he presents us with a world of unchanging, eternal essences, floating above the apparent contingencies of history; producing a curious (if familiar) combination of historical positivism and a covert Platonism which reifies concepts and dissolves history into an eternal now. However, to have assigned a work to a genre does not *precede* interpretation, rather it is *already to have interpreted*.[19] Cairns also avoids any recognition of what we might call 'the politics of genre'. We might instance Ode 4.2, where Horace encodes a public/private dichotomy within generic distinctions between grand and humble lyric, in order to celebrate Augustus' regime. Genres need not be reified, but can be understood discursively, as part of the dynamics of social transaction and communication, and of artistic practice.

The frames within which reading occurs, *and must occur*, become, on this view, provisional, pragmatic, heuristic and contingent, means of controlling textual indeterminacies by establishing agreed procedures and goals. We cannot operate without them, but we can constantly (re)make and unmake them and thereby the possibilities they open up or close off. The danger arises when they become naturalized or otherwise

---

[17] Harrison (1985), 15, 21.

[18] Cairns (1972), 32. My objection here (as elsewhere) is not to Platonism *as such* but to its occlusion.   [19] Cf. Michaels (1978), 788.

congealed as (occluded) metaphysical entities (i.e. categories of funda-mental being). For example, the notion that texts have stable meanings may operate as a useful heuristic 'fiction' to facilitate interpretation. But when the resulting tradition becomes unacceptable to enough readers, they may have to initiate an alternative 'fiction', that texts can be appropriated for any position. (It should be clear that I am not making any exception for my own proposals.) It is in this way that we may view the current turn, or return, to the reader, and not as something which could solve all outstanding problems. A written text is a set of marks until a meaning is construed by a reader (in that sense an author is also always a reader); to that extent texts should not be separated from the processes by which their meaning is constituted. Moreover certain obviously institutional readings – like those offered in universities – are connected with issues of power, since rewards (and penalties) are awarded in accordance with whatever is regarded as success or failure in these operations. The academy legitimates itself by identifying 'problems' to which it can offer 'solutions'; the will-to-power to impose a particular reading, and to persuade others of its validity, is thus integral to the whole academic process. Authority is variously inscribed within particu-lar reading practices, which require (for example) the avoidance of 'anachronism' and so forth. Judgements are always socially constituted, and based on 'an invocation of shared values and public beliefs'.[20]

But problems remain, with readers no less than with (other) contexts.[21] For example, constructions like that of 'a competent reader' (who decides?) or 'an implied reader' (always already a matter of interpreta-tion) seem to amount to little more than the critic himself in another guise. It is hard to discover what readers 'really' think (whatever we take that formulation to mean), especially since any questions we ask have agendas already written in them. Any division between immediate response and reflective critical activity is likewise easily deconstructable. Accounts of reading usually have little to say about minute-by-minute readerly reactions (boredom, distraction, etc.), or the connections we make between a particular text and other areas of our lives (often quite outside the public domain). Accounts of readers thus tend to oscillate between the 'ideal' and the 'historical'. Since interpretation is a socially informed activity, the notion of 'an interpretative community', with

[20] Michaels (1978), 787.
[21] See Moore (1989), 106–7 for a brief but trenchant critique.

shared assumptions, methods and goals, a notion associated above all with Stanley Fish, the leading American proponent of 'reader-response criticism',[22] seems an obviously useful one. But we soon encounter problems of definition. Are we talking about small groups of readers – e.g. radical feminists, deconstructionists, Fishian readers etc. – in which case these are not wholly isolated but overlap? Or of readers within larger periods – Elizabethan readers, Augustan readers etc. – in which case how are the periods to be delineated? How far can there be dialogues between different communities? Is Shakespeare part of 'our' community, or of another community? Is Fish guilty of 'the ideology of communities'? Accounts of readers can be redescribed as competing stories about reading.[23] The Fishian reader, who constantly modifies her understanding of sentences as she reads (as a result of adjusting her sense of their grammatical and syntactical relations) never seems to learn, but is always amazed by the next example of the text's 'self-consumption'. Fishian reading has, in that sense, a narrative shape: surprise, leading to re-structuring, issuing in self-discovery. Problems like these are debated, with particular vigour, within feminism. What does it mean to read 'as a woman', especially if gender is taken, not as something biologically determined, but as tropical and textual?

Texts, we can say (following Derrida), have a capacity for reingrafting themselves within new contexts, and thus remaining readable. As Derrida has it: 'Every sign, linguistic or non-linguistic, spoken or written (in the current sense of this opposition), in a small or large unit, can be *cited*, put between quotation marks; in so doing it can break with every given context, engendering an infinity of new contexts in a manner which is absolutely illimitable'.[24] In this way texts ensure their 'iterability' (though this formulation erases the agency involved) in a process of 'dissemination'.[25] In the light of this, instead of treating texts as having more or less fixed meanings located firmly within partly recoverable backgrounds, which help to explain them, we could negotiate the possible connections which can be constructed between texts, yet with an awareness that this involves a constantly moving 'fusion of horizons'. Every reading of a work becomes a fresh 'instantiation' with its own

[22] For the doctrine *in nuce* see Fish (1980), 3: 'the reader's response is not *to* the meaning; it *is* the meaning.' Fish (1989), 68–86 easily disposes of Iser's view that readers fill up gaps and limited indeterminacies in otherwise determinate texts ('Why no one's afraid of Wolfgang Iser').

[23] Culler (1983), ch. 1, especially 64–83 (65–9 on Fish). [24] Derrida (1977), 185.

[25] Cf. Felperin (1990), 95–9, 121–30; Culler (1983), 121–34.

character (as we can see, for example, from our own re-reading of books at different periods of our lives). The process of *re*contextualization was already in motion with the text's first receivers, so that there never was an obviously fixed original context. Rather each work becomes an intervention within an intertextual field, which, however much it tries to stake out a position, never wholly succeeds in doing so, and whose meanings are constantly realized anew at the point of reception.

If we now return to the Gadamer–Jauss model of reading outlined in section 2, with its stress on the necessarily *historical* nature of understanding, we can see more clearly what I have already suggested is its principal defect. For this model does not, in the end, relinquish the comforting 'metaphysics of the text', that movement towards ideality, of which (in theory) it is suspicious.[26] The text, despite the interpretative movement within time, oddly 'remains the same work'.[27] The problem here may be clarified if I return to my musical analogy. A musical work only becomes such when it is realized in a performance (whether this is a public performance, or a private reading of the score 'in the mind's ear'). Every performance is different from every other performance. A performance of a Bach concerto conducted by Wilhelm Furtwängler differs from one conducted by Christopher Hogwood in tempi, in phrasing and articulation, in pitch, in the number and type of instruments used, in the notes themselves. We may dislike either, or both, but we can only do so by presenting, or positing, a rival realization. No musical performance, even one directed or sanctioned by the composer, could be definitive for all time; indeed composers perform their own works differently on different occasions. We should think then not of a series of more or less imperfect embodiments of an hypostatized perfect performance (a Platonic 'idea') but of a set of performances (some more satisfying than others to particular listeners), displaying 'family relationships'; but nonetheless involved in an unceasing movement of *différance*. And the signs themselves will not serve as grounds, since signs are meaningless unless 'read', realized, and anyway the signs will differ in different editions of the score, which indeed give only very approximate indications to a performer. (Analogously a carefully paragraphed and punctuated modern text of an ancient author, quite unlike an ancient text in presentation, can be seen as an appropriation, a making familiar, and

---

[26] But contra Graff (1985–6), 122: 'in Wittgensteinian terms, this assumption [that interpretations may be predetermined by what they purport to be interpretations *of*] is built into our language game.'   [27] Gadamer (1975), 336.

also, necessarily, an interpretation. The operations of *différance* are already at work in the very (re)constitution of the text.) A concerto by Bach cannot then be 'the same', but has to be involved in a process of differing, for where can that 'sameness' be located? Even a recording cannot stay the flux, for the effect of listening to a performance by Furtwängler today is different from the effect of listening to it at some earlier time, and indeed it is not the same 'I' who listens. So too with a verbal text. A set of signs becomes a poem when it is realized by a reader, who thus acts as a 'performer'. She will have to decide innumerable details of phrasing, rhythm, sound, tone, syntax and so on, and in that sense we cannot draw a firm distinction between reading a poem and offering a (critical) reading of it. Every reading is different from every other reading; once again there is no text-in-itself, but only a series (potentially endless?) of competing (or complementary) readings. Is a poem, in other words, better thought of as *an event (in time)* than as a thing?

4 Telling stories about the past

All current approaches to reading involve, at certain points, historical claims of some kind (we are all historicists now). But there are many histories, and many competing stories about history. History can be seen as a socially embodied, socially negotiated *practice*, constructed discursively. In situating a 'literary' text within history one is therefore negotiating between (at least) two different 'codes'. Any attempt to define history is subject to the rejoinder that such definitions are essentializing, and that, within them, power is being negotiated and distributed, with winners and losers (feminists would argue that women have been among the principal losers, since, in the now notorious word play, history has been, primarily, his story). One of the most influential definitions, Aristotle's in the *Poetics* (1451a 5–7), marked out (despite the somewhat dismissive attitude to history) a distinct area for historical writing, legitimating in theory the practices of Herodotus and Thucydides already inscribed by them in a new category, and projecting this enabling distinction – enabling at least for history-writing as a separate praxis – into the future. History, defined in some such terms as Aristotle's, was, is, or can be a useful category to think and work with, contingently. Anyone who wants to call herself a historian clearly has to draw the line somewhere between what she assigns to 'history' and what to 'non-history';[28] the decision will not be without its rationale, but it can – and will – be represented as defective from other positions. Such decisions, shall we say, are 'always and never' arbitrary. In antiquity there were already arguments about whether Lucan's *Pharsalia* was a 'poem' or a 'history' (both terms, of course, subject to constant slippage); accordingly we have to decide whether Lucan's work 'fails' because it does not fit the existing categories, or whether it would be better to worry about, renegotiate, redefine, or abandon the categories themselves. In other words the *Pharsalia*, to an unusual degree, destabilized the categories operative at the time of its composition, and continues to do so, in so far as we share, or think we share, in those categories today. Classics of 'history' are not infrequently relocated, as a result of institutional activities, as 'literature', another (sliding) discursive category.

We may distinguish, for heuristic purposes, two opposed conceptions of history. Most students of ancient history remain committed to a version of historical enquiry which could be termed positivist, empiricist, referential and realist. According to this model historians scrutinize the 'facts', and interpret them according to rational procedures, to give progressively more accurate accounts of the past 'as it really was'. Of course few would put it as baldly as that, at least in their explicitly methodological statements (where, that is, they make them). They would concede the problems and deficiencies of 'the evidence', the necessary areas of darkness, the diverse way the data can be interpreted. But something not unlike the position I have outlined could be said to underlie the *practice* of many of these historians and above all the style(s) in which they present their 'findings'. There are a number of objections to this model. First, in view of the development of various relativities, together with the 'linguistic turn', it can be argued that there are no 'plain facts' because what counts as a 'fact' is established in discourse, and facts are always already 'under description', always already interpreted. Thus even to use the name Actium, an ideological signifier operating in the interests of 'Augustus' to valorize his new state, is already to be partly complicit with an Augustan account.[29] Similarly structures of temporality, both wider chronological schemes and basic conceptions of time itself, are not 'natural' but cultural variables, conventionally organized. History, it could be argued, is generated by such chronological structures, since dates fix events in relation to other events. In general there is

[28] Cf. Patterson (1987), 44.
[29] Cf. Fish, 'Rhetoric', in Lentricchia and McLaughlin (1990), 203–22, esp. 213.

nothing outside the discourses of history by which accounts of the past can be tested or checked. There is no independent access to historical 'reality' outside the discourses which constitute it. Again historians put the 'past' to the question from the 'present'; since they use the language and concepts of their own day, they could be said to be engaged in an act of translating the past into the terms of the present in a 'fusion of horizons', and translations are, as we shall see in chapter 4, 'different' from the 'texts' translated. So too a piece of historical writing is necessarily teleological, since past events have to be seen 'in the light of the end'. But this is to impose a closure (always and never arbitrary) on the contingent and continuing processes which constitute historicity. Finally, despite the occasional disclaimer, most historians remain committed to a discourse of motives and causes. They are constantly reconstructing, confidently, the motives of historical figures; Augustus' designs, for example, are regularly construed as like those of a modern statesman or politician, as these are taken to be. Even when historians admit that Roman conceptions of character may have been different from ours, instead of allowing that Romans might be substantially alien in their modes of self-construction, they assume that ancient writers are describing the same phenomena as modern writers but less convincingly. So too with causes; as Nietzsche observed, there is a sense in which effects always *precede* causes, since we have to identify an 'event' before we can look for its cause.[30] Even if we accept the validity of a discourse of causes, there will always be an endlessly regressive chain of causative factors inevitably, and, from other perspectives, arbitrarily cut off at some point; events are, in that sense, massively over-determined.[31] Only in the structures of stories can a clear system of cause and effect, action and result, beginning and end – in short, of closure – be inscribed.[32] 'We had the experience but missed the meaning,|And approach to the meaning restores the experience|In a different form.' History is a 'mode of experience', a *praxis*: history is what historians do.

Opposed to this positivistic approach is one which might be termed textualist, post-structuralist, conventionalist, culturalist, anti-foundationalist. On this model history – the past – is an 'absence', and can never be restored to a full presence. It is only available to us in the form of

---

[30] Culler (1981) 183–4, and (1983), 86–8.

[31] Cf. Veyne (1988b), 178: 'Historians . . . do not explain events . . . They explicate them, interpret them'; also Felperin (1990), 150–1.

[32] Cf. Kermode (1967) *passim*.

'traces', first and foremost perhaps in the language we use, and then in the other 'texts' which surround us. Past actions always have to be represented – *under*-represented – in a linguistic or other textual medium. Historians offer us different representations, *re*-presentations, redescriptions, and there are no extra-textual grounds for disputing their rival constructions. As Barthes put it in a famous essay, 'The sign of History from now on is no longer the real, but the intelligible'.[33] History then could be described as 'constructed intertextuality': history is 'a kind of storytelling towards the present, that is, a textual construct at once itself an interpretation and itself open to interpretation'.[34] In this sense all history, whatever truth-claims it may make, is, and has to be, equally textualist: history is something *written*. So I offer my own provisional description of history: *it is a discourse constituted by the traces produced by différance which are present in all textuality.*

One implication of any textualist account is that history always involves troping and figurality, as Hayden White in particular has argued. If history is a story, it requires a plot, and one of White's key terms is, precisely, 'emplotment'. Histories, as he puts it, are 'fictions of factual representation' (the title of one of the essays in his *Tropics of Discourse*). The 'facts' are presented in a style which constitutes a particular interpretation. Histories involve the emplotment of material into different sorts of stories: 'in both [fiction and history]', he writes, 'we recognize the forms by which consciousness both constitutes and colonizes the world it seeks to inhabit comfortably.'[35] On this view rhetoric, within White's practice, is once again privileged over logic and philosophy, and history subordinated to rhetoric, while style becomes inseparable from meaning. The way the story is troped is thus decisive for explanation. In Thucydides events are encoded against an opposition between 'word' and 'deed'.[36] In *The Roman Revolution* Sir Ronald Syme takes details from ancient writers, 'facts' always already interpreted, and re-emplots them within his narrative, where, as in his models Sallust and Tacitus, irony is the dominant mode of troping. Inevitably White's views have met with considerable opposition. His critics accuse him of introducing a disabling relativism, of weakening the notions of 'fact' and

---

[33] Barthes (1981), 18; cf. Bann (1990), 56–63.
[34] Felperin (1990), 144, 159; for *under*representation 51. Both this and the previous section owe a great deal to this book.
[35] White (1978), 99. For a development of these views see Kellner (1989).
[36] Cf. Bann (1990), 55.

'reality', and of undermining the truth of his own meta-historical discourse. To which White replies that he has not deserted 'truth' and 'fact', but reconceptualized them: the point is not that all historical narratives are equally valid, but that they are all equally rhetorical.[37] 'Truth' is anyway a property, not of the world, but of sentences within specific discourses. In the words of Richard Rorty: 'Only descriptions of the world can be true or false. The world on its own – unaided by the describing activities of human beings – cannot.'[38] And we could argue further that truth is made, not found, and made within textuality. There is nothing, it should be added, in the textualist approach to deny that events happen, or that people write books, or suffer, nothing to deny the materiality of the world. But, as Paul Veyne has it, 'The materiality of the gas chambers does not automatically lead to the knowledge one can have about them.'[39] The question is rather an epistemological one, how and in what sense we know those events, those people, that material substance.

In calling history a story, I am not seeking to downgrade it, rather the reverse. We might modify 'there is no outside-text' to 'there is no outside-story', since most language-uses either constitute stories, or at any rate imply a story. Human beings define themselves by the stories they tell as well as by the company they keep. We can only contest one story by telling another. Understanding things means telling stories about things. In stories we (re)make and remake what we call ourselves and what we call the world. In stories we engage in the adult equivalent of the pleasurable play of the child. In stories we repair the damage done by our sense of our own and the world's imperfections, and of our loneliness. Stories speak in and through us. A marriage, for example, tells a story, both personal and social. In theological terms storytelling is the prime act of secondary creation, and in sociological terms it integrates us into our culture, while also allowing us to interrogate it. Stories encode values, and our accounts of stories are always value-laden. The minds we use to judge a story are themselves constituted by other stories (when Wayne Booth talks of 'unnarrated life', he invites the response that life is *always already* narrated[40]) as well as by the story we are 'judging'. Value can be seen as 'counterfactual', but so can most of the other things we most prize: love, friendship, honour, beauty. Value is nonetheless deeply inscribed in the language we use. There is no meta-language in which we

[37] White (1989), 31–6.   [38] Rorty (1989), 5.   [39] Veyne (1988a), 107.
[40] Booth (1988), 14 (but cf. 33) and on story 40–1.

could describe a value-free system. As a result any denial that some stories are better than others collapses in on itself. To seek to avoid value is to court only silence and ultimately madness. It would thus be easy for the textualist to represent the positivist as the enemy of culture and therefore of humanity. In the Judaeo-Christian myth the desire to be God is the sin of Satan.

The textualist story of history is not, of course, invulnerable. One of the commonest criticisms is that it cannot account for historical change. But 'metaphoric redescriptions' would change the world if what contitutes 'the world' is regarded as a matter of description; in Rorty's words 'a talent for speaking differently . . . is the chief instrument of cultural change.'[41] More damaging is the point that each of the two contrasted approaches, at some point, always makes an appeal to the other; they are, in other words, two sides of the same coin. And this has important implications for literary interpretation. As Felperin puts it, 'at a certain level, the historical text must always offer itself, and be received, as timeless and universal textuality even as it remains at another level remote and specific historicity – *if it is to be interpreted at all*.'[42] But when we are within sight of the abyss, it may be a good strategy to essay another path, accepting, with Heidegger, that, for better or worse, language is 'the house we live in', and remembering too that there are many truths, some of them incommensurable. So we can end with a proclamation: 'History is dead – long live history.'

> Every phrase and every sentence is an end and a beginning,
> Every poem an epitaph . . .
> We die with the dying:
> See, they depart, and we go with them.
> We are born with the dead:
> See, they return, and bring us with them.

5 Firing the canon: tradition or treason?

The interlinked ideas of tradition, a canon of approved authors and the classic (a work of proven quality and value, which has stood 'the test of time') remain important within Gadamer's conception of reading

---

[41] Rorty (1989), 16, 7. This is also part of the answer to Fish's claim that theory has no consequences; cf. Smith (1988), 221, note 28.

[42] Felperin (1990), 14. For the Heidegger quotation 53.

historically. The question of the canon has recently generated debate, often acrimonious, both within and outside the academy. The 'radical' critique of the canon hinges on the claim that canons imprison us in the past – 'the tradition of all the dead generations weighs like a nightmare on the brain of the living,'[43] as Marx put it colourfully – and thus in undesirable past values (patriarchal, racist, imperialist etc., and, one might add, 'Marxist'). So, for example, Terry Eagleton, for whom Gadamer's tradition is simply 'a club of the like-minded',[44] sees the formation of canons as one means whereby local ideological interests are given the status of eternal values, the gap between past and present is elided, and 'literature' is depoliticized by an occlusion of those constraints and cultural processes which determine the nature of its discourses. 'We make texts timeless by suppressing their temporality.'[45] Classics can serve as icons, totems, in the interest of the powerful. The very notion of the classic, it is gleefully pointed out, was based on analogy with property qualification (the word was first used of writers by Aulus Gellius, and meant 'a first-class and tax-paying author, not a proletarian'[46]), and classics were employed in schools to teach 'correct' speech and grammar to rising elites. Canons are constructed, as a source of authority, and we ought to look carefully at the processes of their construction, to determine who chooses, and why, and to whose advantage. Canons, in short, on this account, are sites where hegemony is encoded and reproduced.

We must, I think, attend seriously to these charges. Within defences of canon and tradition there is frequently a conservative political agenda, either open or, more commonly, concealed. Geoffrey Strickland, after a defence of the humanist pursuit of 'objective truth', and a claim that the canon 'has created itself' (notice the suppression of agency), writes revealingly: 'it is more than ever necessary to point out the advantages of sharing not only a common humanity, but, within this, a common *imperium*, with its language and common culture, as distinct from the warring tribalism that precedes and follows the rise of empires.'[47] Eliot's influential and still valuable defence of tradition was part of his attempt to vindicate a Roman, Christian and European identity against tenden-

---

[43] Quoted by Patterson (1987), 56 (from *The Eighteenth Brumaire*).
[44] Eagleton (1983), 73. It is tempting to respond with a *tu quoque*.
[45] Smith (1988), 50. For other critiques of traditional notions of tradition see Jauss (1982), 673–6; Weimann (1984), 609–88.
[46] Curtius (1953), 249–50.   [47] Strickland (1991), 36.

cies towards what he termed 'provinciality'. 'We are all', he wrote, 'so far as we inherit the civilization of Europe, still citizens of the Roman Empire.'[48] Anxieties about what it means to be a 'Westerner' or a 'European' (here cultural/ideological signifiers) are thus frequently located within arguments about tradition and canon. E.R. Curtius, for example, found in the idea of the *topos* a stable base for Western culture, whose renewal he sought after the devastation wrought by Nazism (but analogues can be found *outside* the Western tradition for many of these *topoi*); in Curtius' account the *topos* is, unsurprisingly, reified and separated from cultural politics. Eliot's model of tradition also contains traces of idealism (great literature 'composes a simultaneous order'[49] rather than being embedded in culture). Power and authority are likewise at issue. Canons are not infrequently constructed by poets who insert themselves into a tradition in such a way as to seem a valuable addition to it, or even its *telos* (Virgil, for example, does this in the *Georgics*, which gathers together the whole spectrum of previous 'didactic literature', Greek and Roman). Institutions are also involved in the formation and transmission of canons, and, quite apart from an element of sheer inertia, have an obvious interest in maintaining aspects of the *status quo*: teachers of literature who have themselves been trained within a certain tradition tend to wish to perpetuate it.

The charges can, however, be countered, and a more positive view of the uses of the canon developed. First, we may ask whether it would in practice be possible to operate without a canon of any sort: 'given the finiteness of personal existence and of institutional authority, there must be agreed economies.'[50] Canons are needed to preserve disciplines (some disciplines might be better not preserved, of course), and can sustain communities (the role of the Hebrew Bible in maintaining a sense of Jewish identity during periods of persecution would be an obvious instance). Inscribed in the radical critique seems to be an opposition to institutional and cultural authority *in any form*.[51] Moreover there is no reason why canons should be regarded as necessarily, or intrinsically, conservative, since texts can be appropriated for different positions.

---

[48] Eliot (1957), 130 (from 'Virgil and the Christian world').

[49] Eliot (1975), 38 (from 'Tradition and the individual talent').

[50] Steiner (1989), 64.

[51] Cf. Rorty (1989), 64: Foucault 'still thinks in terms of something deep within human beings, which is deformed by acculturation'.

Milton, for instance, used his knowledge of the classical tradition to *challenge* the values of the ruling elite. Even with Eliot canons operate in a dynamic, not a static way; when a 'really new' work is produced, it alters the whole of the tradition.[52] For Eliot tradition (however much he may reify the concept and erase alternative accounts) is, we could say, a structure of differences,[53] not merely a list of approved authors. The relationship between canons and cultures can likewise be seen as a dialectical one: a canon both produces, and is produced by, cultural formations. We may ask too whether canon-making can usefully be reduced to an issue of power alone. Indeed any denial of the canon could just as well be represented as an instance of a will-to-power, since it exalts the role of the critic or theorist (students read Eagleton instead of Milton).[54] Canons can instead by seen as sites where rival claims are registered and where narrowly local interests and tastes can, on occasion at least, be transcended.[55] An ecclesiastical canon (often assembled by councils) may be fixed, though it will generate commentary and diverse interpretation (moreover it did not harm (say) the dissemination of St Augustine's works that they could not be included in the Bible); but secular 'literary' canons are always renegotiable. In Elizabethan grammar schools there was something close to a national curriculum; at St Paul's, for example, in 1580 the list of authors approved for study comprised Terence, Cicero, Caesar, Sallust, Virgil, Horace, Ovid, Valerius Maximus, Seneca, Persius, the younger Pliny, Juvenal, Quintilian, Silius Italicus, and similar lists exist for many other schools.[56] This is a rather less restricted canon of classical authors than ours, but it also excludes some writers widely studied today, in particular Lucretius, Catullus, Propertius. Catullus, who rose to such prominence in the nineteenth century and who was greatly admired in Southern Europe from the sixteenth century onwards, was less popular in England, partly perhaps as a result of the more conservative nature of English humanism (he was not in the medieval canon); only one edition of his works was published in England before 1700, and only in 1702 was there an edition

[52] Eliot (1975), 38.
[53] This conception of tradition as a structure is criticized by Bruns (1991), 11, but his own definition ('tradition . . . is just the historicality of open-ended, intersecting, competing narratives') is so broad that nothing could slip through the net. Cf. Weimann (1984), 76.   [54] Weinsheimer (1991), 134.
[55] Weinsheimer (1991), 126–7.
[56] Baldwin (1944), 1 (415–28 for the Paul's system).

by an English scholar.[57] Above all – to return to my initial point – canons make the past 'usable', amid a contestation of meanings (and thus of futures). Past texts are too extensive; they have to be ordered so that history can be made manageable and evaluated. Canonicity is required, if the past is to be studied at all. Canons, as Kermode points out, thus allow for modernity, creating 'out of the indeterminate, disject facts of history, a core of canonical memory; out of history value'.[58] In the terms of Eliot's *Four Quartets*, we can redeem the past by the use we make of it.

In Eliot's sense of tradition past and present exist in a changing dialectical relationship, in which the present illuminates the literature of the past as well as vice versa. This dynamic concept can usefully be extended to the processes of evaluation themselves. What Barbara Herrnstein Smith terms 'the dynamics of endurance' involve 'a series of continuous interactions among a variably constituted object . . . and mechanisms of cultural selection and transmission'.[59] C.S. Lewis, who, a decade before Jauss's programmatic lectures which launched reception theory in Germany, had proposed a switch from writers to readers' responses, has an eloquent page on the vagaries of 'taste' and fashion: '"Taste" in this sense is mainly a chronological phenomenon. Tell me the date of your birth and I can make a shrewd guess whether you prefer Hopkins or Housman, Hardy or Lawrence.'[60] The often-made claim that the greatness of particular texts is demonstrated by 'the test of time' is hard to reconcile with these vagaries. Hume, for example, illustrating his claim that 'taste' is grounded in 'nature', wrote: 'Whoever would assert an equality of genius and elegance between Ogilby and Milton, or Bunyan and Addison, would be thought to defend no less an extravagance than if he had maintained a molehill to be as high as Teneriffe.'[61] Unfortunately history tends to undermine this appeal to normative agreements, as in the case of Hume's second example. The superiority of Bunyan to Addison would seem as self-evident to many moderns as the reverse did to Hume. And we operate within a necessarily limited time-scale; we have simply no way of knowing whether Shakespeare or Ovid will be read in 500 years time.

---

[57] For Catullus' *Nachleben* see McPeek (1939); Gillespie (1988), 84–89; Wiseman (1985), 211–45.

[58] Kermode (1988), 146. Kermode is constantly returning to the linked issues of canon and institution: see Kermode, (1975) and (1979) *passim*; (1988), chs. 7 and 8; (1988), pt. 2; (1989), ch. 9. Cf. the essays in Von Hallberg (1984); Gorak (1991).

[59] Smith (1988), 47.   [60] Lewis (1961), 105.   [61] Quoted by Smith (1988), 57.

Reception theory will allow us to steer a course around both the radical and the conservative positions. Any talk of tradition negotiates the discursive space generated within the poles of 'change' and 'continuity', 'difference' and 'sameness'. As Alastair MacIntyre puts it: 'Those texts to which . . . canonical status is assigned are treated both as having a fixed meaning embodied in them and also as always open to rereading, so that every tradition becomes to some degree a tradition of critical reinterpretation in which one and the same body of texts, with of course some addition and subtraction, is put to the question, and to successive different sets of questions, as a tradition unfolds.'[62] So too one can argue that the intersection of the contingently time-bound and the transhistorical is precisely where such works of art are situated, *and have to be situated*, if we are to talk coherently about them at all. (One might guess too that part of the reason why 'Shakespeare', say, remains a 'classic' is the unusual openness of his works to the traces in the language.) In terms of the hermeneutics I have been defending, *a classic becomes a text whose 'iterability' is a function of its capacity, which includes the authority vested in its reception, for continued re-appropriations by readers.* As a result of these appropriations the works so appropriated become richer as they are projected through history, because more 'voices' have made themselves heard within them. In this way reception theory can reconcile tradition and culturalism with progress in an empowering synthesis.

MacIntyre has in general made tradition his master-term. Tradition is, to him, an 'historically extended, socially embodied argument',[63] and coherent judgements are made, and can only be made, from within some tradition or other (tradition thus operates like 'discourse' in Foucauldian accounts), since there is no disinterested position outside-tradition from which to operate. We have to recognize this if we are to understand, and make coherent, our present disagreements, and not appeal to some reified, 'liberal' conception of 'Reason' supposedly ungrounded in any prior set of assumptions. The mere possession of a list of 'Great Books' will not of itself bring that coherence:

> It is not of course that such texts are not important reading for anyone with pretensions to education. It is rather that there are systematically different and incompatible ways of reading and appropriating such texts and that until the problems of how they

[62] MacIntyre (1988), 383.
[63] MacIntyre (1985), 222; and see Martindale (1992b).

are to be read have received an answer, such lists do not rise to
the status of a concrete proposal. Or to make the same point in
another way: proponents of this type of Great Books curriculum
often defend it as a way of restoring to us and to our students
what they speak of as *our* cultural tradition; but we are in fact the
inheritors, if that is the right word, of a number of rival and
incompatible traditions and there is no way of either selecting a
list of books to be read or advancing a determinate account of
how they are to be read, interpreted, and elucidated which does
not involve taking a partisan stand in the conflict of traditions.[64]

(Here we see how MacIntyre shares with 'radicals' a recognition of the
necessary interestedness of all discourse, seen as perspectival and
rhetorical *all the way down*.) This is an attractive approach, but it
prompts an obvious objection. How do we identify a 'tradition' without
gross reification? How do we decide where one tradition begins, and
another ends? Whether to stress continuity within change, or breaks with
continuity? This is where we encounter again the ideology of periodization, of categorization. If we retain the notion of tradition as a useful
one but reconstrue it as plural, then conceptions of what is rational and
valuable will change *within* the same tradition as well as between different
traditions. In sum the notion of tradition – because of the differences
within the term – can easily be destabilized, and can only be sustained,
like all other such descriptions, by an 'act of will'. Nonetheless we may
decide to retain the notion, on pragmatic grounds, because of its
empowering character. What matters will then be not whether a tradition
really exists, but whether people are able to position themselves within
what they see as commensurable modes of enquiry. Tradition then
becomes not a thing but a way of conceiving the character of an
intellectual programme, or a body of texts, or whatever.

6 Recovering dialogue

Throughout the centuries many thinkers have stressed the importance of
dialogue in our experience of the world. According to Martin Buber,
human encounters should be construed as encounters of an 'I-Thou'
type, which register the claims of the 'Other', in contrast to objectivist

---

[64] MacIntyre (1990), 228; cf. (1988), 386.

models of knowing, which reduce 'Thou' to 'It'.[65] For both Gadamer and Bakhtin our encounters with texts assume this character. According to Bakhtin the reading process operates within a social context of competing voices and modes of discourse (this polyphony of co-existence, interaction and contestation he called 'heteroglossia'). The 'I' who reads is the locus of dialogue, the text a focus of dialogical processes of production, reception, appropriation. A 'text' is thus a mosaic of voices with specific and different cultural histories whose meaning is controlled by the particular contexts-of-their-use; in this continual exchange 'an utterance is never *in itself* originary',[66] and likewise no utterance will ever be final.[67] Indeed the self is itself dialogic, and thus a person 'lives by the fact that he is not yet finalized'.[68] In Bakhtin's words: 'There is no first or last discourse, and dialogical context knows no limits . . . At every moment of the dialogue, there are immense and unlimited masses of forgotten meaning, but . . . as the dialogue moves forward, they will return to memory and live in renewed form . . . Nothing is absolutely dead: every meaning will celebrate its rebirth.'[69] Accepting our contingency, we can negotiate the world, from where we are, by probing it dialogically, within, or through, different modes of experience.

Reading is often treated as a straightforward communication between a writer and a reader. So Tennyson, in his poem 'Frater Ave atque Vale' (1883), records how close he felt to Catullus when on a visit to Sirmio (ironically the 'Roman ruin' to which he refers is of imperial date).[70] But any claim to be in direct contact with an author, unless we take it as a heuristic fiction to enable interpretation to proceed, seems to be predicated on an unacknowledged metaphysical principle (what deconstructionists call 'the metaphysics of presence'). Further problems reside in disagreements about what constitutes a 'person' in the first place. Ancient philosophers frequently saw the person primarily as a moral agent, influenced by circumstance but capable of self-reformation; Freudians stress the role of the unconscious (structured, according to Lacan, like a language); poststructuralists conceive of de-centred persons who inscribe themselves, or are inscribed, within pre-existing subject-

---

[65] Gadamer (1975), 322–3; Holquist (1990) *passim*; Todorov (1984), especially chs. 4 and 7.
[66] Holquist (1990), 60; cf. Leith and Myerson (1989), 162: 'Language forbids pure origination.'   [67] So e.g. Bruns (1991), 10–12.   [68] Morson (1991), 214.
[69] Quoted by Todorov (1984), 110.   [70] Text in Gillespie (1988), 87.

positions (on this view we are partly a product of the grammar we use). In *Inferno* 5 Francesca tells the story of the beginnings of her adulterous liaison with Paolo:

> We read one day for pastime of Lancelot, how love overcame him
> . . . when we read that the longed-for smile was kissed by so
> great a lover, he who never shall be parted from me, all trembling,
> kissed my mouth.   (127–36)

Dante here shows how a book might relate to an action. The key, on this interpretation, lies in the description of the two kisses, the first described in 'courtly' language which creates a glossy atmosphere of romance, the second insisting on sheer physicality; instead of the 'longed-for smile' (*disiato riso*) a fleshly human mouth (*la bocca*). The lovers, in other words, adopt the subject-position of two famous literary figures, in what could be appropriated as a story about the modalities of appropriation, and this (in Dante's view) destroys their capacity for morally rational judgements and actions. Certainly we may agree that we have no access to sexual experience outside the discourses of sexuality. Such experience is part of the symbolic order, and not simply dependent on biological difference: our sexuality is always *inscribed*. So, in Horace Ode 4.1, which can be read either as a poem about the experience of falling in love again or as a poem about resuming the writing of lyric, the paradoxical elision of sex and text shimmers through the climactic moment of self-revelation (33–6); the significance of being tongue-tied in love only registers because of the existence of an eloquently written discourse of desire. On this view the person is, we could say, 'textualized'. In Barthes's words, 'This "I" which approaches the text is already itself a plurality of other texts, of codes which are infinite or, more precisely, lost.'[71] Indeed if human life is regarded as radically cultural, then the distinction between 'life' and 'representation' partly dissolves, since 'life' becomes, precisely, the experience of cultural representations.

This might suggest that if reading is like getting to know a person, this should not be construed as having a relationship with an author outside or beyond the text, but with an author who is (in Derrida's phrase) 'an idiom which constructs itself in language'. The text can be read, in the author's 'absence', 'non-presence', because meaning is constituted, not

---

[71] Barthes (1974), 10–11.

in author's absence

within consciousness, but within textuality.[72] The gap between texts and persons can thus be closed, but in the opposite direction to the one more often taken; people are like texts in that we encounter their gestures, words and actions, but have no direct access to the full presence of their minds and consciousness. And just as human relationships are matter of value, so meaning and value are inseparable – to discover meaning is to experience value.[73] On this view authors themselves are 'effects of *différance*', and in consequence they become 'iterable'.

There are distinct advantages in conceptualizing the reading process in this way. Reading would then be, not simply a matter of 'decoding' meanings, but rather *an encounter*.[74] As with people, so with books, both the subjectivist and the objectivist reveal a desire to dominate, the one by imposing *his* (supposedly subjective) meaning, the other by imposing *the* ('true') meaning. A complete lack of trust, a complete nihilism about the possibility of understanding, also becomes difficult, or at least hardly a viable human option. Seeing through books, like seeing through people, may make it impossible to see, for people are evidently not wholly ours to command. Like people, books would have their reticences, their partial disclosures, their resistances to complete appropriation; they would invite us to respect their otherness. What we often call 'imagination' in a writer could be like another person's habitual way of construing the world.[75] Trusting another's comments, we could, for example, use our own experience of being discriminated against to understand other forms of discrimination. Understanding would be, not a matter of 'identifica-tion', but a matter of 'approximation'.[76] And we are aware that, with people, there is always more to be known, other ways of experiencing them than our own. We would have to steer a course between total determinacy and total indeterminacy. Successful dialogue partly involves delimiting meanings within a specific context; radical indeterminacy, a very different phenomenon from *différance*, would collapse into total non-communication. In general 'nothing is more frightening than the absence of answer'.[77] But in practice the human mind seems to be

[72] So Harrison (1985), 15–16; cf. Gadamer (1975), 260: understanding is not 'a mysterious communion of souls, but a sharing of a common meaning'. See the introduction to Martindale and Hopkins (1992) for a fuller exposition; Harrison (1991), 188–218.

[73] Mitter (1987), 29 for this formulation.   [74] Cf. e.g. Booth (1988), 70–1.

[75] So my two-year-old son, on seeing a green carpet flecked by sunlight, exclaimed 'cucumber'.   [76] So Todorov (1984), 108; Steiner (1989), 175.

[77] Bakhtin, cited by Todorov (1984), 110.

constituted so that it can, given the opportunity, learn to grasp, or accommodate itself to, symbol systems other than its own, partly, it may be, because these systems constitute structures in which one term illuminates another. And this is so even if the activity of these terms involves *différance*. Or rather it is because of such deferral that a text belonging to one set of cultural codes can fit, more easily than we might have expected, into another. Understanding between two people, it has been suggested, could be like the relation of tenor and vehicle in a metaphor, which creates extension and enhancement in a two-way process.[78]

Of course there are problems with this model of reading, as with any other. There is a danger of excessive optimism about the possibility of fruitful dialogue. Conversations frequently collapse, and there can be losses of readability (for example, many Western-Europeans no longer have a sense of the universe as God's book). Dialogue tends to become, in these accounts, an abstraction which elides the constraints of power, the voluntary and imposed suppressions which conversation can be said to enact.[79] Bakhtin makes the concept of dialogue so all-embracing as to run the risk of emptying it of analytic power: if everything is dialogue, nothing is. And modern critical theorists simultaneously unfix the person, and yet rely for their own communications (if they are to be so regarded) on some residual notion of fixity. In MacIntyre's words: 'A piece of writing, whenever it confronts a reader . . . does so at a time which is not only 'now' for that reader . . . but becomes the author's coincident 'now' . . . In that shared time, exempted in some respects, although not in others from the temporal separation of the 'now' of utterance from the 'now' of reading . . . the timelessness extends to the standards of reason-giving, reason-accepting, and reason-rejecting . . . This appeal . . . is . . . only to be understood adequately as a piece of metaphysics'.[80] To some of these problems we shall be returning.

This notion of dialogue also has implications for the nature of language. Language is often, and usefully, described as 'a signifying system', a system of 'arbitrary' signifiers. But such a description could imply that language is primarily instrumental, that language is a form and meaning a mental activity, and that words operate like numbers; and to this extent it has not freed itself entirely from an 'Enlightenment' belief

[78] Weinsheimer (1991), ch. 4: 'Metaphor as a metaphor of understanding'.

[79] I owe this formulation to Duncan Kennedy.

[80] MacIntyre (1990), 45.

in an abstract 'rationality' outside culture and tradition. It has, in short, residual elements of unacknowledged idealism and covert Platonism.[81] In one sense a word is evidently an arbitrary signifier: what we call 'horse', the Romans called *equus* (given the necessary degree of slippage). But in another sense the arbitrariness of the signifier is only trivially true. For the language-user – except, of course, Humpty-Dumpty in *Through the Looking Glass* – the signifier is never arbitrary because it is always located within a cultural matrix, and thus inextricably connected with use and history. Because we understand the world through language, because language is the basis of any symbolic order, so language and 'reality', signs and things, are bonded. 'The human world is always already a language world, and for exactly that reason the human word is always and in every case worlded.'[82] Moreover, if language is ever on the move, no language-use is wholly containable within any pre-existing system. Language only exists in use, and thus is always a fresh *event*. It can be argued that some particular language-uses involve an unusual degree of renewal of meaning. This sense of the potential freedom of embodied usage, this feeling of the word's complex rootedness in a disclosed and disclosing history, may be a particular feature of what we call 'the classic'. Hence too the paradox that certain texts from the past can speak to some people with more power than anything else in their continuing conversation with the world.

> The communication
> Of the dead is tongued with fire beyond the language of the
> living,

for those communications have been made important by time and by the history to which they have themselves contributed. 'I began with the desire to speak with the dead . . . I could hear only my own voice, but my own voice was the voice of the dead, for the dead had contrived to leave textual traces of themselves, and those traces make themselves heard in the voices of the living.'[83]

OVER

---

[81] See Weinsheimer (1991), ch. 5, 'A word is not a sign', for much of this argument.
[82] Weinsheimer (1991), 112.   [83] Greenblatt (1988), 1.

Rereading Virgil: divertimento

Every writer creates his own precursors.
                                    Borges

There is no document of civilisation which is not at the same time a
document of barbarism.
                              Walter Benjamin

And that's true too.
                    Gloucester in *King Lear*

I Prelude: the critic as artist

The purpose of this chapter is to explore further, through specific
instances, two propositions advanced in the preceding one: first, that all
readings of texts are *situated*, contingent upon their historical moment,
and thus that *to understand is always to understand historically*; and
secondly, that one useful approach to certain great 'imitative' texts is to
see them as rereadings of the works imitated. The first proposition may
not seem particularly controversial, although in practice many critics,
while acknowledging the situatedness of earlier criticism, employ a
rhetoric which might suggest that, partly because of the 'advances' of
scholarship and partly because of their particular 'insights', their own
writings are substantially free from this supposed 'deficiency'. The
second proposition, however, will require some further preliminary
explication before we can turn to the analysis of particular examples.

One of the most characteristic strategies of poststructuralist criticism is
to collapse traditional categories, and (usually) to follow this by the
construction of fresh ones. As we have seen, this is not because the new

categories will be 'true' where the old were not (all 'findings' require the existence of prior categories, always and never arbitrary, on which they are dependent), or even because the new categories are heuristically superior in any but a contingent or pragmatic sense; rather it is because categories so easily become 'naturalized', and deconstruction is then needed to remind us of their discursive character, their *constructedness*, so that we can, at least in part, control them rather than merely let them control us. For example, Derrida blurs the distinction between 'literature' and 'philosophy' by continually exploring the occluded figurality of philosophical discourse; in this way he undermines any claim that philosophers can offer us, in language of transparent referentiality, non-emotive, context-free, non-perspectival accounts of how-things-really-are.[1] This occlusion is one of the means by which 'the Enlightenment project', once designed to challenge authority, can itself be appropriated as a particularly insidious mode of authority. Against 'Reason' (as previously against 'Tradition' or 'Custom') there can be no appeal. Deconstruction at its best is thus a mode of *defamiliarization*, designed to provoke us into fresh apprehensions of fresh possibilities of meaning and to rescue us from what George Steiner terms 'the sloth we call "common sense"'[2] (at its worst it is rather a set of stock moves and tropes and repetitive gestures).

One of the most fundamental of such categories within literary enquiry is the distinction between the creative artist, author, writer on the one hand and the critic, exegete, commentator on the other. Harold Bloom, in his massively influential *The Anxiety of Influence*, partially collapses this apparently primal distinction. According to Bloom all readings are '*misreadings*', either 'strong' or 'weak'. Strong misreadings are principally effected by poets who both exploit and distort the work of their predecessors in a powerfully executed interpretative 'swerve'. And here Bloom appropriates a Freudian paradigm whereby the poet–son displaces the authoritative father-figure, whether quietly or violently, in an attempt to create imaginative space for himself (and yes, writers within this discourse are very definitely 'male'). Bloom's version of literary history thus might seem rather overtly 'mythic' in comparison with more humdrum conceptions of the past: we watch titanic figures wrestling as it were in a void. On this view criticism, necessarily 'belated', can be redescribed as a sort of prose-poetry, and poetry as a sort of verse-

---

[1] See Norris (1983), preface, 1–3.   [2] Steiner (1989), 199.

criticism (Bloom's own writings would be a good example).[3] Now a claim that all readings are misreadings, misprisions, certainly need not imply that 'anything goes', or that all readings are purely subjective or of equal interest and value (clearly Bloom has unusually strong preferences for some readings). Rather it can point to a particular way of conceptualizing the interpretative process, namely that any interpretation, unless it is mere tautology, must be a *re*-stating, and thus necessarily *different* from whatever is interpreted; it is in that sense that all criticism can be described as allegory, as a-saying-in-other-words. Often indeed criticism concerns itself, rather obviously, with filling what are felt as 'gaps', with the 'not-said' of the text, as in the case of so many discussions of characters' motives (for example, the question of why Hamlet delays). Criticism can then be represented as another telling, another story to explain a text, which thereby enacts a particular closure, or series of closures, on that text, but which in turn opens itself to further interpretations. Where those stories are particularly memorable or persuasive or effective in some way, we can talk of a 'strong' misreading (or better perhaps (mis)reading). Bloom himself writes:

> All criticisms that call themselves primary vacillate between
> tautology – in which the poem is and means itself – and reduction
> – in which the poem means something that is not itself a poem.
> Antithetical criticism must begin by denying both tautology and
> reduction, a denial best delivered by the assertion that the
> meaning of a poem can only be a poem, but *another poem – a
> poem not itself.*[4]

Here it may be useful to supplement Bloom's idea of misreading and swerving with another post-structuralist concept, that of *supplementarity*. The meaning of a word or a text is never completed, but always contains a supplement. The signifier is so charged with an excess of energy that it generates further fictions, fictions which serve to answer unanswered questions, fill 'gaps', explain perceived 'contradictions', provide sequels and allow for appropriations in view of new circumstances. Ends of works, in particular, are unstable and subject to supplement. The *Aeneid*, for example, however much it may seem to afford a complete reading of history, mobilizing the resources of both the Greek and the Roman traditions to make the triumph of Rome and

---

[3] Bloom (1973), 94–5.   [4] Bloom (1973), 70.

Augustus seem inevitable, not only allows but even provokes a sequel or sequels. History did not after all stop with Augustus, a point made eloquently by W.H. Auden in his poem 'Secondary Epic', the conclusion of which draws attention to the irony whereby the 'last' Roman Emperor in the West was named, precisely, Romulus Augustulus.

The former Yale deconstructionist J. Hillis Miller reads Sophocles' *Oedipus the King* as a story about the dangers of imposing interpretative closure.[5] *Oedipus*, it has often been observed, has a plot analogous to that of a detective story, with Oedipus as both investigator of the crime and its perpetrator. In the end Oedipus forecloses on his story, when he proclaims its meaning, its *telos*, and blinds himself. The story of his past which he has written proves his undoing. But no story is ever finished, no meaning is ever final, as the existence of first *Oedipus at Colonus*, and then of innumerable reworkings of Sophocles' story, testify. Fictions always mean *more*.[6] In that sense the often-made distinction between 'open', indeterminate texts and 'closed', determinate ones can usefully be dissolved. Worries about closure have led to numerous attempts, in modern and postmodern fiction, to leave the story 'open', but such fictions cannot escape being parasitic upon previous narrative patterns: *a refusal of closure can itself be seen as a dialogue with closure.* The terms closed and open, in other words, are complicit with each other: no closure need be seen as complete, because a sequel is always possible and because gaps can be opened even in the most determinate structures, but equally no text can be treated as wholly open, since, if it were, it would be uninterpretable, meaningless.

This supplementarity can also help to account for the process of continued interpretative revision. Frank Kermode and others have rightly stressed the importance of biblical hermeneutics as an analogue and model for the activities of 'secular' literary criticism.[7] The stories of the Old Testament, for example, were supplemented by *Midrash*, commentary on canonical scripture, which helped to keep the originals available for contemporary needs. There is no end to the stories we can tell about stories, even if what we can know – and instantiate in stories – is

---

[5] 'Narrative', in Lentricchia and McLaughlin (1990), 72–4. It can be argued that the end of *Oedipus the King* itself points to its openness, both in the mention of another oracle for which the characters must wait (1438–1514) and in the entrance of the sisters/daughters, which opens up another category of relationship for anxiety. I owe this point to Denis Feeney.   [6] For this formulation Steiner (1989), 82.

[7] Kermode (1979); and (1983), prologue, 24–5 on this 'hermeneutical increment'.

limited by our contingency. These Midrashic stories, which could be seen as allegories, are ways of 'Saving the Text',[8] although at the same time the text is always also subversive, resisting complete and final appropriation. Steiner nicely catches the paradox of this: with Rabbinic exegesis, he writes, 'in dispersion, the text is homeland', but also such commentary, constituting 'marginalia to the abyss of meaning' is 'an act of exile'.[9] To interpret a text is always to speak *otherwise*. 'Understandable being is itself different from itself'.[10] In that sense allegory could be seen not so much as a quality inherent in certain texts traditionally called 'allegorical' as a function of reading, although, of course, we may accommodate our writings, with varying degrees of success, to particular reading practices which may, or may not, be continued over time.

Attempts like Bloom's to dilute the difference between artist and critic often arouse charges of arrogance. Traditionalists regard criticism as a second-hand, second-order activity, in no way comparable with the productions of artistic genius (though exceptions are often made in the case of a Dr Johnson or a Coleridge). Indeed the matter is subject to a Bloomian analysis, in which the critic, anxious about his secondariness, his belatedness, tries to displace the artist, the envied or hated father-figure, who is the very source of his authority. But there are analogous dangers with traditional approaches too. The 'humble' critic, serving his master the transcendental creative artist, becomes priest or mystagogue, expounding *the* true meaning of the work to the community of the faithful, and not infrequently issuing fatwas or denunciations of the errors, or heresies, of rivals. In Kermode's acerbic words, 'at this point . . . the orthodox . . . man the walls with their dusty banners: principle, imagination, the human world, though the most vocal of them are manifestly unacquainted with the first, lack the second and seem to know the third only by hearsay'.[11] At least Bloom wears his vanity openly on his sleeve. Criticism of all kinds is subject to analysis in terms of 'a will-to-power'. And anyway writing and reading are always 'ensnared in each other'.[12] A complete separation of powers is never possible, even were it desirable.

[8] So Bruns (1991), 10; similarly Jameson (1981), 10: 'Interpretation is here construed as an essentially allegorical act which consists in rewriting a given text in terms of a particular interpretive master code.'   [9] Steiner (1989), 40–1.
[10] Weinsheimer (1991), 122 and cf. 82–6.   [11] Kermode (1983), prologue, 7.
[12] Caputo (1987), 118.

2 Breaking the well-wrought urn

According to a classic interpretation, increasingly criticized but still tenacious in its influence, there is a tension throughout the *Aeneid* between optimism and pessimism. And one of the most seductive statements of this view is to be found in Adam Parry's elegantly written essay, 'The Two Voices of Virgil's *Aeneid*', which was first published in *Arion* in 1963. According to Parry the tension is articulated in terms of two 'voices', a public voice of celebration and an elegiac private voice of lament. Parry's essay can just as easily be 'situated' as any poetic response, and his interpretation depends just as much on certain paradigms which are local and contingent (in this case partly those of the so-called 'New Criticism') and just as much subject to ideological analysis. However – unlike the more openly 'interested' rereadings of Dante and Lucan which we shall be considering later – the essay partly masks its positionality behind a validating scholarly rhetoric. We may start by unpacking aspects of this rhetoric, in order to bring to light some of the buried assumptions of Parry's argument.

Parry starts by identifying a passage which, in his view, gives 'the essential mood of the author', a passage which he finds characteristically 'poignant' and 'Virgilian'.[13] It is the languidly resonant one, drenched in pathos and in nostalgia, in which the Italian landscape mourns for the dead Umbro (7.759–60). To privilege a couple of lines in an epic of approximately 10,000 as a sort of key to the whole is a revealing index of the critics's 'taste'. (By contrast we may infer from Suetonius, *Aug.* 40.5 that one of Augustus' favourite lines was *Romanos rerum dominos gentemque togatam*, 1.282, 'the Romans lords of the world, the people of the toga', which points to a rather different set of values.) The passage evinces, in Parry's opinion, 'something of what used to be called the lyric cry'. This preference for the 'lyrical', characteristic of the New Criticism, could be related to Parry's choice of key interpretative metaphor, that of poetic 'voices' (and why two?), in place of (say) the notion of different

---

[13] Parry (1966), 107–8. Subsequent quotations (in order) are from 109, 110, 111, 110, 112, 109. Compare the elaboration of this approach in the Harvard 'pessimists' and in Lyne (1987). Part of my point is that interpretations which we might agree in calling 'good' (or 'right') are just as historically situated as are 'bad' (or 'wrong') interpretations. Thus Parry's 'fetishization of the aesthetic', even (or especially) where it is in accord with a fetishization which others (including Virgil?) might find in the *Aeneid*, is still also implicated in New Critical discourse. I owe this formulation to Stephen Hinds.

'readings'. How useful is this particular heuristic fiction, and what implications does it have for interpretation? The notion of 'voice' as a linguistic construct, that is the sense of a poet speaking to a reader or some other interlocutor, is commonly found in modern discussions of lyric poetry and grounded in a 'metaphysics of presence'. Frequently, as in Parry's essay, it is linked to a fairly strong version of intentionalism. The 'private' voice of the *Aeneid* is connected with Virgil's own (partly suppressed) feelings about the cost of Empire, which supposedly conflicted with his desire to celebrate the achievements of the regime, but, in another sense, co-exist with it in a kind of higher unity. Likewise the polar categories of 'public' and 'private' are treated by Parry as something unproblematical, but, like all other such categories, these can be represented as not given in nature but constructed in discourse, and therefore always contestable and contested and subject to slippage. The line between the categories must be drawn somewhere, but can always be *re*drawn. For example, is the lament for Marcellus, Augustus' designated heir, (6.868–86) to be attributed to the private or to the public voice? We might remember, too, that a main plank of Augustus' attempt to restore the Republic was legislation regulating 'sexual choice', whereas in many versions of modern 'liberalism' sexual behaviour is largely treated as a private matter. In all such binary oppositions one term tends to dominate the other in a relationship of (potentially) violent hierarchy (e.g. man/woman), and in liberal ideology the private is frequently privileged over the public as more 'authentic', often with the implication that law should be applied as little as possible to the private sphere (cf. the debate over abortion).

In Parry's essay we can discern not only this preoccupation with Virgil's supposed inner feelings, but also the phenomenon sometimes called by theorists 'the fetishization of the aesthetic', that is the construction of a discrete and mystified aesthetic sphere above historical contingency and the mundane world of politics and ideology, what Parry calls 'an artistic finality of vision' which Virgil and we can contemplate with 'the purer emotions of artistic detachment': 'It is as if Virgil were telling us that the way to resolve our personal sorrow over the losses of history is to regard these losses in the same mood as we would a beautifully wrought vessel of clear glass' (cf. the title of Cleanth Brooks's influential *The Well-Wrought Urn*, a classic of the New Criticism). Similarly when Aeneas views dolorous scenes from the Trojan War on the temple gates of Carthage (1.441–95), he sees them, according to

Parry, 'as made beautiful and given universal meaning because human art has transfigured them'. Indeed, with an irony that is perhaps unperceived by the author, the *Aeneid* is described, precisely, as 'a poem . . . about the *imperium* of art'. In all this we might ask if 'sensitivity' is not itself being fetishized, and whether avoidable, or even unavoidable, human suffering ought to be made bearable in quite this way: 'Do not go gentle into that good night'. Does the eloquent pathos of the *Aeneid* (if it is that) reconcile us to human pain, as in the lovingly-evoked deaths of Euryalus or Lausus, and in a rather sinister, aesthetized way?

Parry's liberal reading offers itself as post-imperial, and could be geared in to a growing hostility to the failures of American imperialism in South-East Asia and elsewhere during the 1960s and 70s, but, from another perspective, it could be represented as itself complicit with imperialism. We might argue that the *Aeneid* pre-empts objections to ruling others by making Empire a lonely burden with pain and suffering as the only reward. And here we might recall that a note of noble and resigned melancholy seems to be characteristic of much of the most admired imperial literature; it is common, for example, in the writings of Tennyson and Kipling. Could Parry's essay, in other words, like the *Aeneid* itself, be read as a subtle *apologia* for Empire? But this would require reconceptualizing the terms in which the pathos and multivocality of the *Aeneid* are perceived and described. Barthes was fond of reminding us that it is not so much ideology we have to guard against, as the means whereby it masks, effaces itself.[14] It is therefore interesting to find Parry somewhat blithely invoking a local American parallel for the events of the *Aeneid*: 'his [Virgil's] feeling for them [the original Italian stock] had something in common with what Americans have felt for the American Indian'. The American Indian could indeed be idealized as an image of pristine and uncorrupted primitivism, but this did not save her from annihilation or confinement to reservations: '"I weep for you," the Walrus said:|I deeply sympathize" . . .|Holding his pocket handkerchief|Before his streaming eyes|. . . . But answer came there none –|And this was scarcely odd, because|They'd eaten every one.'

In the end, I would argue, such two-or-more-voices accounts trivialize the *Aeneid* by refusing to take it seriously as a massively influential ideological vehicle. When, in 800 AD, a king of the Franks was crowned, exactly, as *Roman* Emperor, this *translatio imperii* was accompanied by a *translatio studii*, including the study of the *Aeneid*, still one of the most

---

[14] E.g. Barthes (1973), especially 109–59.

seriously demanding investigations of Empire in Western literature. None of this is to make a plea for a return to 'political' criticism alone, or to defend the methodologies of the New Historicism, which is increasingly taking on the appearance of a rising hegemony. Such a political turn in turn has its dangers if it wholly denies the possibility of any fruitful aesthetics. It is to our advantage to retain a series of competing discourses to challenge and interrogate each other, rather than to collapse them into a single master-discourse. The slogan 'everything is political', useful as it may have been as a provocation, is a self-deconstructing one, since it brings with it the implication that 'everything' contains other categories which we could name. Otherwise it would be mere tautology: 'the political is the political'.

3 Dante-reading-Virgil

At the end of *Purgatorio* there occurs (in my story) what might be described as a 'Bloomian' moment. Dante has arrived at the Earthly Paradise, accompanied by Virgil, who, in Hell, had been a revered teacher, guide and source of authority, but who now, in Purgatory, which is outside his previous experience, (and in that sense already in breach of the 'rules' which govern Dante's afterlife), has become more of a loved companion and (increasingly otiose) father-figure. At this point Dante is granted his first sight of the risen Beatrice, riding in a triumphal chariot, the central figure in a magnificent procession, 'the unread vision in the higher dream'. He turns to Virgil in wonder and receives an answering look 'no less charged with amazement' (29.57).[15] A little later Dante turns back again to his master for reassurance, 'with the confidence of a little child that runs to his mother when he is afraid or in distress':

> ma Virgilio n'avea lasciati scemi
>   di sè, Virgilio dolcissimo patre,
>   Virgilio a cui per me mia salute die'mi.   30.49–51

But Virgil had left us bereft of him, Virgil sweetest father, Virgil to whom I gave myself for my salvation.

Immediately afterwards Beatrice addresses Dante by his name, its first (and last) appearance in the poem. Dante, as we say, has 'grown up', and

---

[15] Translations are by Sinclair (1971), slightly adapted. 29.57 is perhaps itself a Virgilian echo; cf. *Aen.* 6.854 *haec mirantibus addit.*

is nearly ready for that vision of Paradise which is far beyond Virgil's vision and which will fit him to be the poet of the *Comedy*. (The *Comedy*, in that sense, is a highly self-reflexive work, for the poem explains how Dante came to write the very poem we are reading.) For all Dante's affectionate reverence for his 'sweetest father', in the end he jettisons him on his road to full self-realization as a man and as a poet.

The mysterious disappearance of Virgil (where is he bound for?), a Virgil who in Dante's eyes is the master-poet of the Western tradition, is the climax of a process which has been continuing, despite all the expressions of admiration by Dante *personaggio*, throughout the first two *cantiche* and which indeed will not cease even in *Paradiso*: 'the progressive undermining of Vergil's authority'.[16] Many readers of the *Aeneid* have felt that what they perceive as Virgil's stark division of the universe into good and evil undermines the sense of an ultimately beneficent providence and teeters on the brink of a radical religious dualism. Dante dramatizes this, to him disabling, Manicheanism in *Inferno* 8–9, when Virgil alone cannot prevail upon the devils to open the city of Dis, equivalent to Virgil's Tartarus, to the two travellers. This can be read as a rereading of *Aeneid* 6.548–65 where Aeneas fails to enter Tartarus, since 'to no good man is it allowed to tread on the wicked threshold' (563), and where there is a suggestion that the city of eternal punishment is completely impregnable: in the Sibyl's words, 'no force of men, *not even the heaven-dwellers themselves*, would be able to destroy it in war' (553–4). In the *Inferno* Virgil is represented as totally at a loss through his rebuff, and it requires an action of God's grace, in the sending of an angel, to compel the demons to allow the travellers further along their road. God's power over Hell is thereby strikingly reaffirmed. The *Aeneid*'s dualism, if such it is, suggests an uncertainty about confronting evil; Dante by contrast must enter Hell, acknowledge his own evil and face the evil in others, before his ascension into Heaven. The *Comedy*, in other words, is a poem in which evil is conceded but also exorcized and transcended; in Virgil, despite the Stoic–Platonic optimism, deep doubts remain. *Inferno* 8–9 thus represents, on this reading, 'a crucial ideological turning point'[17] after the Virgilian routines in the poem's opening cantos. Redeem the dream.

Elsewhere (for example, in *Purgatorio* 3) Virgil evinces confusion over

---

[16] Barolini (1984), 200–1; cf. Hardie (1984). I owe a number of points in this section to my student Isabelle Burbidge.

[17] Barolini (1984), 204, and for Virgil's mistakes cf. Hardie (1970), 1127.

the relationship between soul and body. This confusion reflects the Platonism of Virgil's philosophical underpinning of his poem in Anchises' discourse (6.724–57). The passage speaks of a Platonic dualism in which body and soul are sharply distinguished and the body regarded as the soul's dark prison (in contrast, say, to the Aristotelian–Thomistic view of the indissoluble linkage between body and soul, espoused by Dante himself). In mainstream Christianity neither the body nor the world are regarded as intrinsically evil (in Genesis God sees that the universe He has created is good), and Virgil's Platonism also sits very uneasily with the view of Rome as the supreme earthly city and of Augustus as a god on earth, which requires rather a doctrine of embodiment or incarnation. Dante focuses on something analogous to what Marxists would call 'contradictions', or liberal humanists 'tensions', or deconstructionists 'fissures', although he does so, obviously, from a very different ideological perspective. Another 'contradiction' is that between Aeneas' dutiful prayerfulness and the character of some of the gods to whom he prays. Dante was apparently so perturbed by the line in *Aeneid* 6 (376) *desine fata deum flecti sperare precando*, 'cease to hope that the fixed decrees of the gods can be turned by praying', that he makes Virgil modify his position in *Purgatorio* 6. Similarly Aeneas' doubts about the gods' concern with justice, so memorably conveyed by his obituary notice for Rhipeus:

> cadit et Rhipeus, iustissimus unus
> qui fuit in Teucris et servantissimus aequi
> (dis aliter visum)   2.426–8

Rhipeus too fell, who was the justest single man among the Trojans and the most observant of the right – the gods thought differently

are flamboyantly contradicted when Dante places this obscure Trojan among the elect in the eye of the eagle (*Par.* 20.68), a pagan redeemed by the operations of Grace before – at least in earthly sequential time – the Incarnation. Redeem the dream.

Dante's very choice of title may have adversative implications. The *Comedy* is so called, in contrast to Virgil's *alta tragedia* (*Inf.* 20.113) because the story ends happily and because it is written in the vernacular (the 'vulgar' tongue) which even women use, or so the *Letter to Can Grande* (para. 10), probably if not certainly the work of Dante himself,

45

affirms. All this connects with what I have called 'the politics of genre', whereby words like 'high' and 'low', words applicable also to social distinctions, are often used in generic contexts. Dante's professed *umiltà* thus assumes an ideological aspect, for example in his assertion that he is no hero (*Inf.* 2.32 'Io non Enëa'). The *Comedy* starts like a dream vision, only to incorporate, with the appearance of Virgil, various epic tropes and Virgilian sequences: it continually both constructs and deconstructs itself as an epic. In the words of the 'epitaph' composed by one early commentator, Guido da Pisa, 'Here lies Dante the lofty comic poet, | And satiric, lyric and tragic poet as well.'[18] In terms of its linguistic range it can encompass everything from the most lofty grandeur, via the street brawlings of contemporary Florence, to echoes of baby talk. Dante's book is thus designed to reflect the book of God, the universe itself, in its variety and comprehensiveness. And this reminds us too that the state of the soul after death is not dependent on earthly social distinctions: 'where there is neither Greek nor Jew, circumcision nor uncircumcision, barbarian, Scythian, bond nor free, but Christ is all, and in all'. The *Comedy* smashes down both the classical genre system and the values which it encodes. Asked about the language of Eden, Adam makes clear to the poet that no one earthly language – not Hebrew, not Latin – can claim priority over others (*Par.* 26). We are all descendants of Babel, and no existing language is more originary or authoritative than any other. Transferred from 'religion' to 'politics' this could have distinctly subversive implications for the social order. And after this our exile.

These 'corrections' of Virgil point to a paradoxical relationship between the two poets, which is susceptible of a Bloomian analysis. On the one hand Dante reveres Virgil almost to idolatry. The *Aeneid* is called a *volume*, not a *libro*, like the universe itself, God's book. Similarly Virgil is *autore*, a source of authorship and authority, where God is *verace autore*, 'true author' (*Par.* 26.40). In this way Dante constructs an image of the great epic poet which in the end he himself will appropriate: in *Paradiso* 25 he says that he will return a poet, *ritornerò poeta* (8). He builds himself into a tradition, conferring quasi-canonical status on himself (e.g. *Inf.* 4), and also tries to control the meanings of his predecessors by his mode of citation, validating his right to criticize them. He is interested, in particular, in Virgil's status as a prophetic writer. In *Purgatorio* 22 Statius explains to Dante how he first became a poet and a

---

[18] See Caesar (1989), 128. And for the generic issue cf. Auerbach (1953).

Christian through his encounter with the writings of Virgil and particularly with the fourth *Eclogue*, a poem widely regarded in the Middle Ages as a prophecy of the Incarnation. Dante's translation here (70–2) shows that he fully understood that *Virgo* in *Eclogue* 4 on one level refers to Astraea, goddess of Justice; but, while conceding this historicist sense, he affirms that Virgil was nonetheless the mouthpiece of the Holy Spirit, with the result that he was 'like him that goes by night and carries the light behind him and does not help himself but makes wise those that follow' (67–9). It would thus be inept to accuse Dante of naive anachronism; it is rather a question of what reading practices are considered appropriate. Dante's handling of *Eclogue* 4 shows that he was not prepared to limit meaning to the likely intentions of the (human) author. (It follows, presumably, that Dante himself, like Virgil, cannot be regarded as a uniquely privileged reader of his own poetry.) However, for all these genuflections to *l'altissimo poeta*, Dante is simultaneously working *against* Virgil's text as well as with it, thereby enabling himself to create his own poem by a Bloomian swerve. The poetic *agon* culminates, at the level of plot, with Dante's destruction of his poetic 'father'. And it is to that moment that, in conclusion, we may now return.

Purgatorio 30 is a densely Virgilian echo-chamber. The threefold mention of Virgil's name, already quoted, has been linked with the analogous iteration of Eurydice in Orpheus' lament in *Georgics* 4 (525–7), a passage of an elegiac plangency unusual even for Virgil. There are two specific Virgilian citations: *Manibus o date lilia plenis* (21), Latin words taken, to greet Beatrice, from the passage in *Aeneid* 6 following the epicedium for Marcellus (883), and *conosco i segni dell' antica fiamma* (48, 'I recognize the marks of the ancient flame') translated from *Aeneid* 4.23 where Dido tells Anna of her awakened love for Aeneas. Virgil is thus evoked, with unusual persistence, at the very moment of his displacement. And all three quotations are from particularly grief-laden passages in Virgil's works. Dante, we may argue, makes clear his attitude to the chill which many readers have sensed in the *Aeneid* when he quotes, twice, from moments freighted with despair, twisting the words to a new meaning to celebrate the joyous epiphany of Beatrice. As for the appropriation of Virgilian grief to grieve for Virgil himself, Dante is sternly interrupted by Beatrice with these words: 'Dante, because Virgil leaves you, weep not yet, for you must weep for another sword.' So Virgilian sorrow receives its rebuke from higher authority, in the name of Love. Dante's implication seems to be that Virgil's inability to reconcile *amor* and *fatum* springs, ultimately, from his paganism, which he partly – but only partly – transcended. In other words Virgil failed to provide an adequate philosophy to underpin his construction of Roman history, and the poem accordingly calls out for revision and transumption. This, it can be submitted, is an impressive reading, a 'Christian' reading of course, but then many of the most fashionable accounts of our day simply attribute to Virgil himself their author's own 'liberal' values, which, by implication, they see as timeless. But there is no escaping our own historicity.

4 Lucan-reading-Virgil

Lucan's reading of Virgil is more markedly adversarial than Dante's. This poetic contest involves a violent displacement of the father, who is indispensable and yet hated. The *Pharsalia*[19] thus enacts a violation of its own life-blood, appropriately enough (it could be argued) in a poem which might well be read under the sign of self-slaughter, both individual and collective. Lucan's disenchantment can show us a way of reading the *Aeneid* which alerts us to the ideological nexus it encodes. By vaunting its own textuality, the poem's paradoxical surface reminds us that all texts are only texts, and that none gives us unmediated access to 'reality' or 'the truth'. The *Aeneid* does not 'reveal' a 'pattern in history', as Gordon Williams has it,[20] it constructs a possible pattern, which we may approve or deplore. And what is constructed can also be deconstructed, and this too Lucan does to all the tropes, sequences and procedures of the Virgilian text. Much of Virgil's material is what we would today call 'myth' or 'legend'. Lucan rehistoricizes the genre, to expose Virgil's partially hidden subtext, in the process collapsing traditional distinctions between oratory, history and epic poetry, to the dismay of some ancient (and modern) critics.

Lucan's anti-Virgilianism is by now a commonplace. His radical revisionism is prefigured in the very first word of the poem. *Bella* caps Virgil's synecdochic *arma* (while also perhaps resonating with the *Aeneid*'s second proem (*Aen.* 7.37–45)): Virgil gives part, Lucan the whole, and the plural 'wars' need not be taken as merely 'poetic', since war in Lucan never concludes, never reaches any Virgilian *telos*, subject,

---

[19] The 'original' title was probably *De bello civili*, but in a book on reception the tradition should perhaps be respected.　　[20] Williams (1983), 5.

rather, endlessly, to deferral, in the perpetual duel between Caesarism and *libertas* (7.695–6). When Lucan comes to describe the pivotal battle of Pharsalia, there is no room for either individual *aristeia* (although the attempt, by a disguised Brutus, to kill Caesar may be a modernist deformation of this particular epic routine) or single combat; in place of individuals slain we are given, and that by means of the figure of *omissio*, a list of typical deaths which climaxes in parricide (7.617–30). The dead are neither named nor lamented, for the horror of this war is too great for Virgilian reconciling pathos, and its significance transcends individual human suffering. Lucan's adjustments to epic diction (including numerous 'prosaisms') also serve to destabilize generic expectations and question the politics of traditional epic style and decorum and the ways in which these are naturalized. Matters of literary classification, as we have seen, always have social or political implications (genres like societies have their 'hierarchies'). More than this, civil war puts language itself under pressure, by highlighting the slide of the signifier against the signified, and reminds us that power struggles are partly about words and how and by whom they are to be used. In John Henderson's formulation, the world at war is also the word at war. We can see more in all this than overt anti-Virgilianism: Lucan can prompt us into fresh ways of perceiving the *Aeneid* which might otherwise have remained invisible to us.

Let us test this thesis by using the *Pharsalia* as our guide to a much admired and discussed passage in *Aeneid* 8, Aeneas' visit to Pallanteum. In *Phars.* 9.961–99 Caesar visits the site of dead Troy, and is led through a bleak landscape heavy with decayed myths by the local cicerone, who tells tall stories to this eminent tourist. Scholars have long recognized the numerous Virgilian echoes in this passage. Lucan turns a number of Virgilian motifs upside down. Where Pallanteum is a type, a prefigurement, of future Rome, Lucan's ruined Troy can be read as a symbol of a world destroyed, echoing the desolation of Italy (1.24–9). Where Aeneas gazes with reverence and wonder at the spot, Caesar tramples on places whose alleged significance he cannot recognize. There is no future of the kind there is in Virgil, no hope – only barely visible traces of a lost past. And after this our exile. As Lucan cleverly puts it, *etiam periere ruinae*, 'even the ruins are ruined' (969). In Latin poetry the traditional contrast between the past and present appearance of a place is normally evocative and glamorous as well as antiquarian: so with Virgil. Lucan, however, drains away the Virgilian resonances; the tone might be termed archaeological rather than romantic. In this Virgilian graveyard Caesar pronounces a prayer which is a kind of summation of the whole Julian myth as celebrated in the *Aeneid*. But the gods to whom he offers *pia tura* (996) preside only over ashes (*di cinerum*, 990), or live in the ruins of the city. Caesar's arrogantly hypercritical and irreligious prayer is in ironic antithesis to the prayers of Virgil's dutiful Aeneas. The typology which links Aeneas and Augustus is thus destroyed or inverted, and with it its teleological implications. Lucan also gives a blackly-humorous, sardonic twist to the *topos* whereby poetry is more lasting than monuments:

> o sacer et magnus vatum labor! omnia fato
> eripis et populis donas mortalibus aevum.
> invidia sacrae, Caesar, ne tangere famae:
> nam, si quid Latiis fas est promittere Musis,
> quantum Zmyrnaei durabunt vatis honores,
> venturi me teque legent; Pharsalia nostra
> vivet et a nullo tenebris damnabimur aevo. (9.980–6)

O sacred (accursed?) and mighty task of bards. You snatch
everything from death, and give to mortal peoples lasting fame.
Caesar, be not touched by envy of sacred fame. For, if it is
permitted (speakable) to Latin Muses to promise anything, as long
as the honour paid to the bard of Smyrna [Homer] lasts,
men-to-come will read of me and you. Our Pharsalia will live, and
we shall not be condemned to darkness by any age.

The potential ironies here ricochet. The passage could be seen as mocking the pretensions of poets to control their own reception[21] (compare Virgil's tribute to Nisus and Euryalus, *Aen.* 9.446–9). We recall how Alexander (for Lucan a type of the tyrant), when he visited Troy, was moved by envy of Achilles, who had found Homer to commemorate his exploits; Caesar, the new Alexander, has received his poet in Lucan. Lucan, displaying a kind of self-loathing and a contempt for a worn-out and compromised epic tradition, links the destinies of the subverter of *libertas* and the poet who records his subversions.

W.R. Johnson sees this episode as a hilarious parody of its Virgilian analogue.[22] Certainly it can be argued that we have here a classic instance of what today would be called 'deformation' or 'demystification'. Virgil opposes the 'pastoral' simplicity of Pallanteum to the grandeur of Rome.

---

[21] I owe this point to Isabelle Burbidge.   [22] Johnson (1987), 118–21.

'Liberal' critics often, as we have seen, conceptualize this opposition in terms of the supposed public/private divide in Virgil's sensibility, and describe the passage as evincing fructifying internal tensions. Lucan's rereading suggests an alternative interpretation. Virgil, we could say, is presenting a vision of the continuing city and (by implication) of the role of Augustus as rightful heir of its traditions. To do this the passage blurs genres, crossing epic with pastoral. Virgil's myth potently mediates, or massages, a necessary 'contradiction' within the spiritual idea of Rome, which is simultaneously the *caput rerum*, the metropolis which Augustus found brick and left marble, and an idyll of primitivism and rural simplicity, sweet especial rural scene. On this reading there is not so much conflict as the (attempted) *erasure* of conflict, in the interests of Roman identity and Augustan ideology. Rome is both an empire of unsurpassed wealth and might and yet, 'at heart', a simple country community. (Compare some myths of modern America, at once superpower and the land of the lone cowboy.) Ideologies, in other words, may hammer together energizing 'contradictions', which are not then felt as contradictions. So Augustus' dominance required both that a transformation of Rome had been effected and that the state of the nation was so terminal that a savour was yet required. Thoughts like this might prompt a more politicized, rather less friendly reading of the *Aeneid* than many offered today.[23] Lucan's relentless unmasking of Virgil's (possible) subtext makes available a very different account of 'the phenomena' which are used to support a multiple-voice reading, whether optimistic or pessimistic.

Here it may be relevant to remark on what we might call the 'ideology of ruins'. Ruins suggest immemorial antiquity, and thus that the present social order is rooted deep in time and the soil; culture and nature are mysteriously at one. So Virgil's magnificent fusions of past, present and future in the landscapes of Italy provide the validation of time for what others have preferred to call Augustus' 'new' state. Claude, in his luminous painting of Aeneas' arrival at Pallanteum now at Anglesey Abbey (plate 1), appropriates this Virgilian fusion for his aristocratic patrons, the Altieri, who claimed descent from Aeneas and whose banner flutters proudly above Aeneas' ships.[24] Claude points us towards an understanding of the possible resonances of the episode comparable with

[23] So Patterson (1987), 160. I owe this point to Catharine Edwards.
[24] See Langdon (1989), 148–50.

Lucan's, yet one of course quite without Lucanian rancour. At the bottom left-hand corner a shepherd and shepherdess sit among their sheep, partly in shade, partly bathed in a rich glowing light, the very emblem of pastoral. By contrast preternaturally elongated, angular epic warriors greet each other from ship to shore, while Aeneas holds up the laurel, symbol of peace. The city on the left, built upon a hill representing the Aventine, gives us glimpses of recognizable classical buildings ('anachronistic' in this context), including the Pantheon, widely regarded at the time as the finest extant example of Roman architecture but also significantly used as a Christian church, a sign of change-within-continuity, of tradition. On the right are the ruins of the older cities, with, between them and Pallanteum, athwart the Tiber, the remains of the Ponte Rotto, which crosses the Tiber below Tiber-island. The blending of genres, the overall harmony of design, the sense of depth and distance in the landscape, the rich and subtle colouring – all create a picture of 'timeless' civility, at once ideal (no such landscape ever existed) and laying claim to a kind of historicity (we can identify particular landscape features and Roman buildings). The princely Altieri family is inscribed within an image of the classical world both modern and venerably antique, to which it becomes the 'natural' heir.

This kind of analysis of the *Aeneid*, which starts by opening and probing fissures within the text, could be described as an exercise in deconstructive reading. Order, including any account of the world or of a book, depends on the maintenance of categories. If deconstruction promised (as it sometimes seems to do) to collapse all categories into an undifferentiated textuality, that would indeed be 'the end of history', in which nothing was open to description and therefore nothing could happen. Significantly accounts of Creation – whether in Genesis or in Ovid or elsewhere – often contain the notion of *separation*, of making ordering distinctions. But whether categories will hold depends partly on the 'will-to-power' of those involved in using them; can they be kept apart? Traditional criticism tends to represent its distinctions as 'natural' or 'rational', concealing any will-to-power. But deconstruction is no less an expression of similar desires, since in practice it sets up new categories which in turn could themselves be deconstructed. Lucan's poem can be used to confront some of these issues. It is indeed a work which could be said to deconstruct itself. In civil war – the *word* at war – power and description are at issue. The ability to construct a narrative and to impose closure and a unified meaning or meanings on history is always already a dispensation of power. Hence a desire in Lucan to avoid narration, a desire for silence (7.552–6). But even silence – as many were to find under the Empire – can be seen as a desire for closure, as an implied narrative. History is not so easily defeated. Even to talk of a return to chaos, of aimless meaninglessness, as Lucan so often does, is to be entrammelled in the world of power, of Caesarism, since 'chaos' is written within a discourse in which 'order' is implied. We are reaching here the limits of the speakable, of the thinkable, and are now, as perhaps we all must be, in a discourse I would want to term 'metaphysical'. Most art helps to conceal the possibility of the abyss from us: Lucan unusually takes us some way towards it. It is no wonder, then, that his text has aroused such hatred and condemnation. But all this is why, for some of us, the wonder-boy's[25] wonder-poem is one reference point for Western poetry.

Finally, one may ask whether Lucan's rereading of Virgil is an unduly reductive one, one which ignores most of what appeals to most admirers of the *Aeneid* today. Certainly it bleaches out much of the Virgilian colour and variety of poetic texture. But is the complex polysemeity of the *Aeneid* something to be admired or deplored? Does it reconcile us to *imperium* and Caesarism, defusing possible objections by incorporating rival viewpoints within itself? To give a final answer would be to revert from reception to a positivistic essentialism. But perhaps for a poet writing under Nero Lucan's may have been the only reading possible. And what of today, as we contemplate our revised visions of a new world-order, *imperium sine fine*, the end of ideology and of history? *Cum domino pax ista venit*?

5 Postlude: the artist as critic

When a student is asked to write an essay on the *Aeneid*, she will normally be encouraged to read some modern criticism, but not often directed to Lucan or Dante or Milton or some other successor-poet to Virgil. This chapter is thus, *inter alia*, a plea for a revised pedagogy. But why should we prefer Dante's or Lucan's readings of the *Aeneid* to (say) Adam Parry's? There are a number of possible responses to this question. First, as I have already indicated, most modern criticism rests on *unacknowledged* ideological and evaluative paradigms, and, at the same time, seeks to insulate literature from challenging us by its appeals to historicism and

---

[25] Kenney (1965) calls Lucan 'a marvellous boy' (299).

to scholarly 'objectivity'. By contrast, both Lucan and Dante take Virgil too seriously to treat the *Aeneid* simply as a piece of 'dead' literature. They recognize that their views of the world are not Virgil's, and yet read the poem without pretending to disattach their own values and sensibilities. As a result a dialogic criticism eventuates. Shall these bones live? Moreover, as Steiner puts it, the successor-poet is 'answerable to the original precisely because it puts at eminent risk the stature, the fortunes of his own work'.[26] So too the stories which Dante and Lucan tell about the *Aeneid* may seem richer and more persuasive, in the particular respects I have been attempting to illustrate, than those of most modern scholars. Again – and this is one of the principal theses of this book – the reception of a text, including the poetic revisions it engenders, is inseparable, in ways that are often ignored, from our current readings of it; T.S. Eliot's Virgil, for example, is in part created by his study of Dante's, and in general, both through Eliot and in other ways, the *Comedy* has left its traces in the *Aeneid* as many read it today.[27]

There is, however, a more fundamental objection. Since (say) Dante's reading of Virgil must (on this view) be *our* reading of Dante's reading of Virgil, that is as situated and contingent as any other account we can give of Virgil – and the same is true of course of our reading of Parry – nothing significant is added by this method of interpretation. One rejoinder is that, if literature is describable as a system of differences, the addition of an extra element always opens up fresh hermeneutical possibilities. Or, more pragmatically, we may say that the readings which result contain 'novelties', and we may find them, in some particular ways we can specify, more adequate to our sense of the 'text'. For example my account of Lucan-reading-Virgil differs in respects from current orthodoxies on Virgil; a space has been introduced for an oppositional view. But difficulties still remain. In the above there have been appeals, from time to time, to the validatory discourse of 'the Author' which a version of reception theory such as I have been advancing seeks, in part, to contest. So, at this point, the argument requires a further twist. Instead of Virgil, 'Virgil', that is *'all-the-forces-that-moulded-the-text-plus-its-reception'*;[28] so too for Dante 'Dante' and for Lucan 'Lucan'. And where can we stop? On this way of reading a 'reader' reads 'Martindale' reads 'Dante' or 'Lucan' reads 'Virgil' . . . Is there any escape from *différance*? 'One understands differently when one understands at all.'[29]

[26] Steiner (1989), 13.   [27] Reeves (1989), especially ch. 4.
[28] For this formulation see Kennedy (forthcoming).
[29] Gadamer quoted in this form by Kermode (1983), 203 (= Gadamer (1975), 264).

3

Rereading Ovid and Lucan: cadenzas

Not occasionally only, but always, the meaning of a text goes beyond its author.

Gadamer

. . . nothing was going to stop Naso's apotheosis now. And so officialdom came to its senses. If, in fact, any one could lay claim to the poet for his purposes, be it a terrorist from the catacombs or some Sicilian peasant and arsonist, why shouldn't true patriots and citizens, law-abiding Rome itself, do the same?

Christoph Ransmayr, The Last World

KING   I have nothing with this answer, Hamlet. These words are not mine.

HAMLET   No, nor mine now.

Hamlet

i Ovid received

The strategy of this chapter is to illustrate, further and through divergent modes of analysis, the contention that, in pragmatic terms at least, one of the most productive ways of approaching certain classical poets can be through the history of their reception as a whole. Both Ovid and Lucan, for example, still suffer rather thin and unrewarding treatment from many scholars today, whereas over the centuries the response has often been urgent and committed. We can thus use the tradition to bypass twentieth-century criticism, to relativize current reactions, and to free ourselves for a more positive approach to their writings. Since Ovid's importance within the Western tradition has been pretty well documented,[1] I shall confine myself to giving two specific examples of responses to his work, both from the Renaissance – one by a writer, the other by a painter – in support of this argument. In the case of Lucan I shall attempt a wider (though necessarily brief and sketchy) picture to suggest that a combination of reception-history with some of the insights of modern 'theorists' produces a 'stronger' reading of the *Pharsalia* than is possible within those approaches more often practised today among Latinists. Here, then, are my stories.

(a) Marlowe–Ovid–Marlowe

The first sestiad of Marlowe's *Hero and Leander*, the best and best known of a number of Ovidian erotic narratives composed during the 1580s and 1590s,[2] plots the initial phases, and delays, in the slowly-developing affair between the two still inexperienced young lovers. At 385 a yet further delay is introduced in the form of a narrative digression, to 'explain' why Cupid was at odds with the Destinies, its digressive character emphasized by the narrator's somewhat Ancient-Mariner-like introductory flourish: 'Hearken awhile, and I will tell you why' (are you sitting comfortably?). Aetiological myths are often treated in modern discussions as pre-scientific equivalents of enquiries into origins and causes to which today we would give scientific or scholarly form. It is arguable that Ovid, as later Kipling, thought otherwise, and that such stories could instead be treated, primarily or wholly, as affirmations of present conditions. The most remarkable feature of an elephant, it might be said, is that it has a trunk. Well, once upon a time it didn't, until the Elephant's Child met his crocodile: 'Led go! You are hurtig be!' Marlowe's invented aetiological myth, which begins with Mercury's seduction of a country maid, could be read, in this light, as a deconstruction both of aetiology and of digression.[3] Instead of a clear structure of cause and effect, of closure, we are offered, in increasingly Shandean manner, a narrative in which any hope of coherent explanation or origin is gradually thwarted. The digression is anyway ultimately (from one point of view) pointless, since it leaves matters exactly where they were before, and serves only to delay – like so much else in Marlowe's poem – the listener's desire for one implied closure, the longed-for consummation of the lovers' love.

---

[1] See Martindale (1988), Barkan (1986), both with further references.
[2] On these poems see Keach (1977).   [3] Cf. Lerner (1988), 133.

Storytelling, in this poem, involves the (willing) seduction of the reader and becomes a focus of desire, one which can never be fully satisfied, but must always be deferred, by the provision of fresh narrative configurations. Significantly Marlowe, for whatever reason, never finished the work (or is even to call it 'unfinished' to imply a *telos*?). Earlier in the sestiad (51-90) the narrator had, provocatively, caressed (in words) Leander's naked body; our desire to hear the story is linked to the desirability of Leander in the eyes of the narrator, and thus the poem becomes simultaneously 'an invitation to love and an invitation to read'.[4] Is appetite the only reality? As the digression becomes more and more digressive, so aetiologies pullulate, of a clumsily handled and cliché-ridden kind (469-82). The narrator's asides and explanations are similarly gauche. The poetic lustre and sustained, if leisurely, narrative power of the main story are altogether absent. The storyteller is perhaps also ignorant of the 'proper' logic of narrative patterns: thus he gives us a sort of inverted *pastorella* in which Mercury first tries rape and only then verbal seduction (a reversal of the 'normal' sequence). At a subsequent point in this shaggy dog's tale the Fates, in love with Mercury, offer him the knife they use to cut the threads of life, and 'at his fair feathered feet the engines laid' (449), a grotesque parody of a love-gift (the weirdly feathered feet are presumably 'fair' to the lovers' eyes). The digression becomes ever more incoherent, until it is with an almost audible sigh of relief that we (and Marlowe) reach the end of this sestiad, and can at last return to the story of Hero and Leander which resumes in the next.

At the outset of the digression Marlowe had referred us to Ovid's story of Io (*Met.* 1.568-747):

> Heaven's winged herald, Jove-born Mercury,
> The selfsame day that he asleep had laid
> Enchanted Argus . . .

We might take this as an invitation to read the Ovidian tale through the eyes of 'Marlowe' as the composer of this curiously ham-fisted Ovidian digression. The story of Io contains its own inset narrative, when, to put Argus to sleep, Mercury tells him the tale of Pan and Syrinx, which in the end, or rather in the middle (for Mercury never finishes it) induces sleep. Poetry and song frequently produce such an enchanted sleep, but the

---

[4] I take this formulation from an essay by Isabelle Burbidge; and cf. Lerner (1988), 129.

story is so flatly told that we might suspect this is rather the sleep of boredom. The narrative pattern – a god essays to rape a nymph who only eludes him by metamorphosing into a plant – is already familiar to the reader of *Metamorphoses* 1 in the deftly turned tale of Apollo and Daphne. But, in this re-run, the various *topoi* and motifs are recycled baldly and in routine fashion. Even the promising comparison of Syrinx to Diana seems to go astray in tangled Shandean fashion (695–7): 'dressed in Diana's style she could be mistaken for Leto's daughter, if it were not that the one had a bow of horn, the other of gold – still even so she was thus mistaken'. At 700 Ovid breaks off the story as told by Mercury (later we learn that at this point Argus fell asleep), and completes it, perfunctorily and in *oratio obliqua*, almost as if he has lost all interest in it.

The mannered 'incompetence' of this 'digression' can, in this case, be read back into the 'main' narrative (this is of course a distinction which the constant turns of the *Metamorphoses* largely deconstruct). The transition from the story of Daphne to that of Io is achieved by means of the description of Tempe, where the rivers gather to console Peneus for his loss (568–82). Normally such an *ecphrasis*, particularly one so extended, would generate a significant quantity of narrative, and would precede, and give emphasis to, an important narrative moment. In this case we instead encounter a swerve, as we slide into the story of Io, whose father Inachus, we are told, alone did *not* go to Tempe. The *ecphrasis* itself is commonly read as an unusually sensitive piece of landscape description (which indeed it is), but it can also sustain a more self-reflexive reading. Groves, woods, waters and caves (and of course Tempe itself) are regularly associated with poetry, and several phrases might recall key terms in the Roman revival of Callimachean aesthetics (*gravi tenues*, 571; *in mare deducunt fessas erroribus undas*, 582). Certainly the story of Io, the woman who turned into a cow, could be seen as archly Callimachean, teasing the reader with generic mixing (*polyeideia*, cf. Callimachus fr. 203 Pfeiffer) and uncertainty of tone (pathos or bathos?). The instabilities serve to produce a series of generic deformations.[5] In 618–20 Jupiter is given a potentially tragic dilemma, a conflict between *pudor* and *amor*, which is immediately and untragically resolved (moreover he is the 'wrong' sex for this particular conflict). Inachus' lament for his daughter (651–63) reproduces a number of 'tragic' and

---

[5] Hinds (1987) sets the terms of the current debate. For the *necessary* impurity of genre see Derrida (1980).

'elegiac' gestures, but these gestures are given a special piquancy by the fact that Io is not dead, but translated into a cow (thus her inability to answer in 655–6 is due, not to her demise, but to her loss of (human) voice). In 668 Mercury is prepared, in grandest style, for epic descent (as in *Aeneid* 4), but his downward flight is perfunctory and anti-climactic, and he is immediately resituated in the 'wrong' genre, pastoral (*ut pastor*, 676), where he smoothly quotes from Virgil's first *Eclogue* (679 appropriates *Ecl.* 1.79; and cf. *per devia rura, capellas, structis avenis, herba, umbram*). Io's conversion into cow-shape has as it were triggered the episode's conversion into bucolic. In the sonorous lament for the dead Argus (720–1), the epic trope of the loss of light in death is deftly adapted to the abnormal circumstance: *Arge, iaces, quodque in tot lumina lumen habebas | extinctum est, centumque oculos nox occupat una* ('Argus, you lie low, and the light you had for so many eyes (lights) is extinguished, and one night seizes a hundred eyes'). As in this instance such deformations frequently generate complex word-plays or puns; so in 743, *de bove nil superest formae nisi candor in illa*, Io's oscillation between woman and cow is reflected in the slide in the meaning of *forma* ('shape', 'beauty') and *candor* ('whiteness', 'loveliness'). Slippages of this kind undermine the security of language, reference and meaning.

Reading back through Marlowe, then, we might see Ovid's Io as a highly sophisticated exercise in getting the story crooked. Such play with genre and *topos* is often treated as a form of wit only, but could have more subversive implications. To map a work onto a 'pre-system' of narrative patterns and onto a generic grid requires the enabling 'fiction' of a system of unified genres and of narrative norms, whereas in practice, we may argue, it is impossible not to 'mix' genres, and stylistic decorum is anyway not fixed but constantly renegotiated. Ovid, of course, frequently plays with such notions of a normative generic system, as he does with so much else; his defence of the *Ars amatoria*, for example, implies that some at least of his possible addressees may believe in such a system. How a work is read will depend in part on whether it is construed, within a particular reading practice, as 'normal' or 'abnormal'. The *Metamorphoses*, generically skewed as an epic, was re-emplotted as a 'romance' by Renaissance theorists like Cinthio, and accordingly became 'orthodox', 'correct', itself normative. Ovid's misfortune (as a man) was that his work was perceived, by readers of authority in his own day, as dangerously 'abnormal'. Such uncertainties extend to the issue of personality; the poem displays the phenomenon of insecure and fleeting identity, 'of a self

... spilling over into another self'.[6] So too, in Marlowe, we are presented not with unified 'characters' so beloved by 'traditional' criticism, but with figures who are constructed by those who view them to become sets of signs in a (conflicting) play of desires, including homoerotic desires (in Leander's case, Hero's, Neptune's, the narrator's, perhaps ours). In short Marlowe's Ovidian *Hero and Leander* could prompt a reading of Ovid's *Metamorphoses* in which genres and personalities are denaturalized, polarities and categories formed and broken down, closure both offered and denied, in dizzyingly vertiginous fashion.

(b) Titian–Ovid–Titian

Titian produced a series of Ovidian paintings, which he called *poesie* (i.e. free poetic evocations rather than illustrations) based on the *Metamorphoses* which he apparently read in Dolce's translation (1553). Inter-art analogies are frequently regarded with suspicion, or treated as wholly invalid. The comparison of painting and poetry, while once serving to raise the status of pictures, is also, it can be argued, locked into a traditional hierarchy of semiotic value, whereby the word is privileged over the image. Paintings, however, can usefully be represented as texts, which always have to be read (there is no 'pure' vision in that sense), according to certain semiotic conventions (though these conventions may be breached, extended or subverted in the process), and an 'educated' reader of Titian's *poesie* could not be prevented from 'completing' the meaning through her knowledge of Titian's 'source' in Ovid. Similarly references to other works of art (like the use of the Laocoon group in Titian's 'Bacchus and Ariadne') operate in a way which is analogous to 'allusion' within literary texts. At all events Titian's paintings can prompt readings of Ovid different from many current today.[7] For example, the story of Actaeon, in Galinsky's view of it, is treated by Ovid in an ultimately unserious way. 'The subject', he writes, 'cries out for a theodicy . . . but Ovid glosses over it in a glib transition.' Any sympathy we might feel for Actaeon is, according to him, dissipated by the distracting bravura catalogue of dogs, the paradoxical and over-graphic description of Actaeon's death, and the trivial discussion it

[6] Fränkel (1945), 99.
[7] Cf. Llewellyn (1988), and cf. Martindale (1988), introduction, 4–5; C. and M. Martindale (1990), 56–7, 65; Wethey (1975), 71–93; Panofsky (1969).

Plate 1 Claude Lorrain, *The Landing of Aeneas in Latium* (1675)

Plate 2 Titian, *Diana and Actaeon* (1556–9)

Plate 3 Titian, *The Death of Actaeon* (1570–5)

Plate 4 Titian, *The Flaying of Marsyas* (1570–5)

provokes.[8] This reading is substantially at odds with the reception of Ovid's story, both in literature and in art, where we continually encounter a response to its darker possibilities. Titian chose to paint what are arguably its two finest narrative moments. In *Diana and Actaeon* (National Gallery of Scotland, Edinburgh, plate 2) Actaeon blunders, unsuspectingly, upon Diana and her nymphs in their grotto. In *The Death of Actaeon* (National Gallery, London, plate 3) Actaeon, now transformed into a stag, or rather stag/man, is torn to pieces by his own hounds, in the pitiless presence of the goddess.

In his *Diana and Actaeon* Titian employs a richer colouring, and displays a greater interest in contrasted textures, than in his previous work. These characteristics can be attributed to the influence of Veronese,[9] but we might see them too as providing a painterly equivalent for aspects of Ovid's text (as Titian may have read it, and as we might read it). Ovidian virtuosity is evident in the catalogue of thirty-three dogs with inventively canine names (206–25), brought to an insouciant conclusion with the words *quosque referre mora est* ('and others whom it would hold us up to mention'). The disproportionate length of this epic-style catalogue has a transgressive effect, as the confusion of the critics suggests. This is the artistry which proclaims artistry. Titian's image too has been read partly as 'a manifesto for the art of painting';[10] for example there is the way that the carvings are reflected in the water below, or that the whiteness of Diana's naked flesh is given emphasis by the contrast with the clothed body of her black attendant, or that her swerve away from Actaeon is represented by the 'unrealistic' fusion of two phases in that recoil so that back and breast are simultaneously seen by the viewer. But the drama of the event is not neglected amidst all this technical display. In particular the brilliant (and sinister?) red hanging, which isolates Actaeon, could be seen as increasing the sense of movement, and heightening the tension with its suggestion of violation. Actaeon's arrival in Ovid is preceded by an *ecphrasis* of the valley and its *antrum* (with its characteristic sense of the sacred) which provides a peaceful backdrop for the violent action which follows (155ff.). Such *loca amoena* are repeatedly scenes of rape in the poem, and, in some versions, Actaeon was indeed guilty of sexual provocation, either as a voyeur or in

---

[8] Galinsky (1975), 66–7, 102–3, 195. A rather more 'postmodern' Ovid has been emerging since 1975, mainly in scholarly articles, but it has not been consolidated as a rival 'orthodoxy', at least in Britain.

[9] So Hope (1980), 128–9.   [10] Hope (1980), 133.

seeking physical union with Diana. But Ovid's Actaeon is 'innocent', and the only rape is the rending of his body which Diana herself instigates, in a powerful displacement of the common sequence.[11] As we have seen Galinsky implies that, had Ovid been telling the tale 'properly', he would have addressed himself to the issue of theodicy in a more concentrated manner and justified the ways of gods to men (one way of defusing Ovid's potentially radical scepticism is to stigmatize it as frivolous or engaged in for merely 'technical' reasons). Ovid's Actaeon is punished, not for any *scelus*, but for a mishap (142), and Ovid later used the story in connection with the *error* which, he claimed, had led to his own banishment by another angry 'god': *inscius Actaeon vidit sine veste Dianam* (*Tristia* 2.105). This might suggest that, *pace* Galinsky, the callous triviality of Ovid's gods has its own power and its own relevance to human experience. Titian's *The Death of Actaeon* is wholly dominated by the massive figure of Diana, at once strangely beautiful and heartlessly indifferent, as, without pity, she attends to her archery while Actaeon is torn to pieces. The figure of Actaeon in the background is a sinister blend of animal and man, hard to discern or make sense of. In Ovid the grotesque nightmare of category displacement focuses on the problem of communication, since the stag's mind remains human (cf. the deliberative questions in 204–5 or the suggestively placed matronymic at 198), yet he/it cannot speak. And Ovid brilliantly exploits the fact that a stag at bay looks as if it might be pleading with its captors (240–1): *et genibus pronis supplex similisque roganti | circumfert tacitos tamquam sua bracchia vultus* ('and suppliant on bent knees and like one beseeching he/it casts round, as though they were arms, his silent looks'). Ovid's destabilization of norms also has its analogues in Titian. In *Diana and Actaeon* Titian may be said to 'deconstruct our notions of "up" and "down" and challenge the "closure" of the classically-composed painting confined within the frame'.[12] Diana, as we have seen, is viewed from in front but from two incompatible viewpoints, in torsion, while Actaeon and the nymphs are seen 'from above', and the trees on the right 'from below'. It matters little what Titian's motives were for this destabilization of space and viewpoint, whether, for example, he was simply taking a distinctly belated interest in those mannerist developments which were so fashionable in Italy outside Venice; the effect is what concerns us, and could be described as 'Ovidian'. The dissolutions of *The Death of Actaeon* are of a

---

[11] Cf. Segal (1969), 42–5.

[12] I quote this formulation from a dissertation by Philip Young, to which I am substantially indebted in this section.

different kind (admittedly the picture seems to be unfinished); the paint is applied thickly and impressionistically, in a restricted range of browns, greens and flashes of yellow-gold, to create an effect of swirling light and movement. Titian is unusually successful as a painter of Ovidian scenes, even if we put this down to a series of inspired 'accidents'. In short, his two Actaeon paintings foreground the violence, cruelty, terror and category-confusion – and beauty – which (on this reading) are key elements in Ovid's account, and thus these (and other) Ovidian paintings can show us that a work of art can be disturbing in its impact while being witty, that in general reductive categories (like 'serious'/'humorous') may make it difficult to do justice to an 'Ovidian' vision. In other words Titian's appropriations of Ovid seem (to some of us) peculiarly persuasive.

The critical problems we have been looking at are stretched to breaking point by the story of Marsyas (*Met.* 6.382–400), which Titian tackled in one of his very last paintings (plate 4). To L.P. Wilkinson Ovid's story displays a taste for 'gruesomeness', and for E.J. Kenney it is 'the ultimate in gruesome wit' which cannot be justified artistically, any more than Titian's painting which it inspired: 'More than one critic has tried to justify the treatment on artistic grounds, just as more than one pundit has assured the world that Titian's picture of the subject offers an uplifting experience to the beholder'.[13] According to Galinsky Ovid revels in the graphic details of torture, which become a vehicle for wit, and shows no interest in Marsyas' sufferings at the human level, reducing the sympathy figure of mourning nature to an empty *topos*. Certainly Marsyas, while being flayed, is made to say, with pointed ingenuity, *quid me mihi detrahis* (385), 'why do you draw me from myself', while Ovid· cleverly observes of his flayed body *nec quicquam nisi vulnus erat* (388) 'it was nothing but wound'. But Ovid hardly offers us a set-piece of Grand Guignol, and indeed the story receives highly concentrated treatment in only nineteen lines. Its haunting character is attested by its massive progeny, and the passage has the capacity to crowd some readers' imaginations; no critical account I have seen even begins to offer any explanation of its curious impact, at the point of reception. Perhaps the ambiguities of Titian's image may prove more helpful.[14] The sense of detachment emanating from all the characters (even Marsyas), the strange serenity of the painting with its muted but sensuous colour and

[13] Wilkinson (1955), 162; Kenney (1986), 411; Galinsky (1975), 134–5.

[14] My discussion owes a great deal to Sawday (1990): quotations from 113 and 130. For pain as the focus of artistic vision see Feeney (1991), 193 n.20.

creamy surface, the thoughtful industry with which – like artists and without seeming brutality – the flayers perform their terrible work, the combination of the impressionistic with precise details like the sharp outline of the skin peeled away from Marsyas' body – all intensify the troubling character of the image. The artist's virtuosity might seem, as with Ovid, to have outrun his human sympathy. One set of ambiguities revolves around issues of power: is the flaying justified punishment, or should we feel sympathy for a victim of authority? – even if the latter we, like the audience in the picture, or in Ovid's story, cannot rescue him, but only 'commemorate' (we are forced to be viewers only). The flaying seems, in Titian, both 'a sacramental . . . act' (in Dante *Paradiso* 1.20–1 the myth is used to image the soul cut free from the body) and an act of callous cruelty (with a sickening suggestiveness as a dog laps up some blood which has not found its way into the bucket set for the purpose). Galinsky suggests that Ovid presents Marsyas' torture 'almost as an anatomy lesson' (and invokes the fate of gladiators and criminals). In Titian the relevance of dissection is still more plausible; Marsyas' upturned body is 'objectified', made the object of a detached but in its way loving scrutiny of a 'scientific' kind, and Apollo cuts it open with the concentrated attention (which in turn arouses concentration in the audience) of the anatomy teacher. In Ovid there is a *frisson* in the contrast between the pastoral setting and the pulsating revealed *viscera*, and the pain is curiously defused in the transition of the onlookers' tears into the clearest river in Phrygia (another displacement, since we might expect the river to have been created from Marsyas' blood). In other words Marsyas' pain is pain aestheticized, objectified, made the focus of artistic vision. But isn't that in a sense what any artistic representation of pain is, and must be? To think otherwise might be to flatter ourselves for our 'sensitivity' as we indulge our emotions over imagined and imaginary sufferings, which could, perhaps, become another (occluded) form of 'the fetishization of the aesthetic'.

2 Lucan restored

There are signs that a major revaluation of Lucan's *Pharsalia* may now, at last, be underway.[15] But it is still hard to imagine a time when poets and scholars weightily debated the rival merits of Lucan and Virgil. The

---

[15] I have found most to interest me in Feeney (1991), ch. 6; Johnson (1987); Masters (1992); and, above all, Henderson (1988).

conservatism of Latin scholarship and its isolation from intellectual developments outside have in general prevented the exploitation of fresh contexts of reception within which Lucan's reputation could have flourished: a revived interest in mannerism and the baroque, for example, or in Jacobean drama, or metaphysical poetry, or developments in Surrealist or Absurdist or postmodern art. (Spanish scholars, heirs to an artistic tradition which includes Goya and Buñuel, El Greco and Gongora, Lorca and Dali, have been able to adopt Lucan, like his uncle Seneca, as a writer with an authentically 'Spanish' sensibility.[16]) Robert Graves, who disliked Lucan, makes an analogous point about Lucan's 'modernism' (i.e. his potential for appropriation by modernists) in the introduction to his translation: 'To poets whom loss of faith in their own national institutions, ethics, religion, and even in themselves, sends marching and counter-marching through the Waste Land, Lucan can be . . . a "standard-bearer"'.[17] But the relative unimportance of Classics today means that such revaluations anyway have little enough impact on the wider culture. It was not always so. The quality and number of Lucan's admirers and imitators throughout the ages might give us pause (as well as pointing to possible ways of reading the *Pharsalia*).[18] They include Tacitus, who (it could be said) shares something of Lucan's mordant political vision, Juvenal, who matches his ferocious declamatory brilliance, black humour and self-lacerating cynicism, Marvell, whose 'Horatian Ode' juxtaposes Horatian and Lucanian accounts of the Roman Revolution, Goethe, who was attracted by Lucan's 'grotesque sublime', and whole cohorts of Whigs, radicals, revolutionaries and Romantics, including Shelley, who introduced Lucan into *Adonais* (his lament for the youthful Keats) and who on one occasion called the *Pharsalia* 'a poem as it appears to me of wonderful genius, and transcending Virgil'. In the eighteenth and early nineteenth centuries Lucanian aristocratic *libertas* proved easily recuperable for modern Liberty and Republicanism. As the Whig writer William Hayley put it:

> Though critic spleen insult thy rougher line,
> Though wronged thy genius, and thy name misplaced
> By vain distinctions of fastidious taste,
> Indignant Freedom, with just anger fired,
> Shall guard the poet whom herself inspired.[19]

[16] So Lloyd-Jones (1990), 39.   [17] Cited by Gillespie (1988), 148.
[18] See Gillespie (1988), 139–49; Martindale (1986), ch. 5; Johnson (1987) remarks *passim*; Due (1962), 77–86.   [19] Gillespie (1988), 146.

By 1782, when these lines were published, Lucan was already under fire for deficiencies of 'taste', including what Hayley himself called 'many a tumid point' which he likened to 'warts projecting from Herculean veins'. And Lucan's bad taste, we are now always being told, is illustrated by his fondness for grotesque violence and horror, for 'rhetoric' and hyperbole and bombast, for lack of all Virgilian 'restraint'. As we have seen, aesthetic statements must be understood within the discourses in which they are constructed and which they help to construct, and while aesthetic judgements are perfectly legitimate, they require rigorous examination, and interrogation, within other discourses, if they are to do more than act as markers of 'distinction' and sustain elites with the warm glow of their own cultural superiority; notions of taste require unpacking to see what concealed cultural assumptions and hidden political agendas they might contain (and certainly hostility to Lucan's politics as perceived, or a refusal to take them seriously – which may amount to the same thing – can often be situated within these adverse judgements). The discourse of 'the natural', for example, is frequently invoked against Lucan. So his characters supposedly talk too rhetorically, too theatrically, to be convincing, realistic, natural. But of course what is regarded as 'natural' is (from another perspective) culturally constructed and constantly shifting. The English*man*'s view of these things has been created, reflected and sustained, above all, in such things as Shakespeare's plays (as usually received) and the 'orthodox' bougeois novel. But, within a Roman context, we can find heated and self-conscious language like that of Lucan's characters in 'life' (that is, in non-poetic texts) too. When Tacitus' Agrippina calls out to one of her murderers *ventrem feri* (*Annals* 14.8), we may be reminded of Jocasta in Seneca's *Oedipus* who kills herself by striking a sword through the womb where she has 'sinned'. Roland Mayer just manages to miss the point: the analogy, he writes, 'shows, in a small way, that a real woman, faced with murder, spoke and thought like a cardboard character from a Senecan play'.[20] Similarly Lucan himself apparently died repeating some of his own verses, presumably an assertion of *libertas* in defiance of Nero who had forbidden him to recite. And Nero's own dying words, according to Suetonius (*Nero* 49) took the form of an epigram (*qualis artifex pereo*). Those whose concept of personality is informed by (say) French classical drama, including Corneille (who significantly preferred Lucan to Virgil), might not so readily make the same response as Mayer.

[20] Mayer (1981), 21.

Lucan's 'bad taste' is frequently illustrated by his 'over-use', or 'abuse', of the apostrophe (what is the 'correct' frequency of apostrophes, one wonders?), which becomes indeed a sort of master-trope within the *Pharsalia*, and which can arouse considerable embarrassment in his modern interpreters. One possible strategy is to ignore the figure; so J.D. Duff's Loeb translation removes numerous instances. To Duff, a typical classical formalist, the use of apostrophe is a convention which has little effect on meaning: 'In Latin apostrophe is often a metrical device, and often a meaningless convention . . . and also the reader is puzzled and confused when Lucan addresses his rhetorical appeal to two or three different persons or places in the same paragraph.'[21] It is hardly surprising to find that, in Duff's view, 'No *reasonable* [my italics] judgment can rank Lucan among the world's great epic poets.' A more productive approach is suggested by Jonathan Culler's discussion of this trope in *The Pursuit of Signs*.[22] For Culler, as for any classical rhetorician, apostrophe is an intensifier, a signifier of passion and emotion, linking the author's voice to the reader and thus constituting discourse as a space between subjects. As a result the poetic voice becomes a visionary voice, which summons 'images of its power so as to establish its identity as poetical and prophetic'. Any direct appeal to persons or things is an attempt to bind them to one's desire, and, as a result, the universe is constituted, by this trope, as 'a world of sentient forces' (as it was in Stoic doctrine). Likewise apostrophe becomes a 'sign of a fiction which knows its own fictive nature', and thus can entail 'an act of radical interiorization and solipsism'. Finally Culler claims that apostrophe is an anti-narrative trope, which replaces narrative by stasis, time by atemporality, 'a referential temporality' by 'a temporality of discourse', so that a text becomes 'a play of presence and absence governed not by time but by poetic power' (I would prefer to say that temporality and narrativity are not so much abolished as reconstituted, recoded). Certainly Lucan's disdain for conventional narrative procedures is well known and often criticized and attributed to the 'decadence' of the age. In the light of Culler's discussion (in which Lucan is never mentioned) we could see a particular significance in the use of apostrophe in the *Pharsalia*, dominated as it is by the free-wheeling, self-lacerating voice of the individual at odds with his world, which he turns into a theatre for himself and his interlocutors, animate and

---

[21] Duff (1928), preface, vi and introduction, x.
[22] Culler (1981) 'Apostrophe', 135–54; quotations from 142, 139, 146, 150.

inanimate. In general the ostentatious textuality of the *Pharsalia* can be contrasted with Caesar's cool, 'classical' prose, or Virgil's poetic 'control' and economy. And here we should avoid attempts to tone down the subversive energies of Lucan's text. Formalist criticism does so by re-emplotting those 'subversions' as 'breaches of decorum', but Lucan's modern admirers too (including my earlier 'self') can be over-inclined to try to fit the *Pharsalia* to traditional models of interpretation based on decorum, the functionality of language, unity of structure. Some of this critical furniture may have to be jettisoned altogether:

> Don't bother to reclaim *this* classic in the name of a 'literature': this text screams a curse on its readers and upon itself . . . in a press of destabilising counter-creation. Non-committal historical placing of declamatory rhetoric, politely appreciative focussing on conceptual artistry, even acutely-attuned response to the power of an unrestrained intellect, these along with the rest of the baggage of your criticism are all by the way.[23]

Perhaps, then, Lucan's poem invites us not to recuperate any notion of 'taste' but to shatter it into smithereens, in order that we can walk naked in the desert. Henderson's voice, in this extraordinary essay, might indeed be compared to Lucan's own. It is wild, accusing, ranting, loathing both itself and what it construes as the 'other'; it *challenges*; it could be described as, in its own peculiar way, profoundly 'religious' – calling us to put on sackcloth and ashes, and walk in the wilderness, and confess our sins – but, at the same time, profoundly atheistical – because there is no-one and nothing to confess our sins to. The classical establishment has a way with such voices, and a number of discourses can be invoked to repress them: the discourse of maturity ('this voice is adolescent, has never grown up'); of decorum ('this is not the appropriate style for an article: opaque, self-indulgent, ungrammatical, meaningless'); of the permanent ('this voice is "trendy", transient, it will go away'); of scholarship ('we may justly praise the worldly-wise, compassionate, many-sided imperialism of Virgil, but feminism, pacificism – irrelevant, not to be adverted to, autobiography not scholarship'); above all of religion ('this is HERESY'). Perhaps the scholars are right, and Lucan and Henderson are simply arrested adolescents who lack the self-knowledge and maturity to compromise with the world and learn its wisdom. But let us imagine, just for a moment, that the scholars

[23] Henderson (1988), 123.

are wrong, that they could be 'celebrating their own security', taking the pain and challenge out of literature, and that, in so doing, they become complicit with many things which are commonsense now, but which future generations will find hard to understand, harder to forgive. In this way we may be betraying the one claim to usefulness which intellectuals might be felt to have. Is that what Henderson-reading-Lucan could be asking us to ask ourselves?

In the light of Henderson's account it may be significant that one of the most creative – perhaps indeed the most creative – use ever made of the *Pharsalia* is in Dante's *Inferno*, that supreme image of a counter-creative world. Dante might well have been baffled by criticisms of Lucan's 'bad taste' and amazed by our neglect of his poem. For him Lucan was *quello grande poeta* (*Convivio* 4.28.13); so impressive was his Cato that he could become a figure for God Himself, and later made into the guardian of Purgatory. In *Inferno* 4 Lucan is among the small group of authoritative epic poets whom Dante encounters in Limbo and with whom (by implication) he claims an equality. And significantly the passages in the *Pharsalia* which seem most to have attracted him (like many other poets) are precisely those so frequently censured in Victorian and modern scholarly criticism, including the Erictho episode and the scene of the snakes in the Libyan desert, which are often cited as examples of Lucan at his bizarre worst. Erictho makes a number of subsequent reappearances in European literature, for example in Goethe's *Faust*, or, thus vigorously realized by Marston, in *The Tragedy of Sophonisba* (IV.i):

> But if dark winds
> Or thick black clouds drive back the blinded stars,
> When her deep magic makes forced heaven quake
> And thunder spite of Jove, Erictho then
> From naked graves stalks out, heaves proud her head
> With long unkempt hair loaden, and strives to snatch
> The night's quick sulphur. Then she bursts up tombs,
> From half-rot cerecloths then she scrapes dry gums
> For her black rites. But when she finds a corse
> New graved, whose entrails yet not turn
> To slimy filth, with greedy havoc then
> She makes fierce spoil and swells with wicked triumph
> To bury her lean knuckles in his eyes;
> Then she doth gnaw the pale and o'ergrown nails
> From his dry hand.   [cf. *Pharsalia* 6.518–43]

Out of the Erictho episode Dante devised a novel fiction (*Inf.* 9.18–27) to explain Virgil's familiarity with Hell's lower depths (his proper space is in Limbo). In *Inferno* 25, in which Dante describes the transformation of some Florentine thieves into serpents, he bids the classical masters of metamorphosis give place (94–7): 'Let Lucan now be silent with his tales of wretched Sabellus and Nasidius, and let him wait to hear what now comes forth! Let Ovid be silent . . .' (Lucan's snake episode also caught the attention of Milton (*PL* 10.410–584) and of Shelley, who alludes to it more than once, most effectively in *Prometheus Unbound* III i 39–41: 'all my being | Like him whom the Numidian seps did thaw | Into a dew with poison, is dissolved.') Ovid is another of Dante's poetic models, but it is Lucan's *terribilità*, in the combination of wickedness and violence and horror and black humour and ostentatious verbal paradox, which seems to dominate in *Inferno*. Dante's chamber of horrors is constructed, to a large extent, out of puns and word-plays; so Bertran de Born, who divided (in one sense) father and son, carries his head divided (in another) from his trunk (*Inf.* 28.118–42). Dante appears to have grasped that parts of the *Pharsalia* can be read as a form of sardonic humour, something which, among modern critics, only W.R. Johnson and Jamie Masters have recognized.[24] One example must suffice: in 4.37–43 Lucan describes a surreal, paradoxical non-battle *on the vertical*, an instance of the sort of cartoon-style joke which, in its 'silliness', serves to undermine epic pretensions and offend the sober-minded. But 'restraint' is not always a virtue. The 'good taste' of Virgil had served to glorify Caesar Augustus; perhaps the destruction of Rome and the loss of liberty required, not good taste, but rather deformation of taste and of the literary tradition. In such a world theodicy gives room to counter-theodicy. George Granville, Lord Lansdowne, hostile though he was to Republicanism, understood the point very well. Criticizing one of Lucan's most celebrated *sententiae* (*victrix causa deis placuit sed victa Catoni*) he wrote: 'Success implies permission, and not approbation; to place the gods always on the thriving side, is to make them partakers of all successful wickedness . . . Lucan was a determined republican; no wonder he was a freethinker.'[25] Not that Lucan's 'atheism' is lacking in bitterness, or anxiety. The gods are a powerful presence in the *Pharsalia* precisely *because of* their absence, which leaves a gap where traditionally there had been a source of authority, the word spoken, *fatum*. 'He has not

---

[24] Johnson (1987) e.g. 56–8; Masters (1992), 56–8, 180.
[25] Cited Gillespie (1988), 145.

abandoned the gods, they have abandoned him.'[26] Without them the poet can only spiral down an abyss of encroaching non-meaning.

Masters has argued, brilliantly, that the *Pharsalia* contains both a 'Republican' and an 'anti-Republican' poem, and linked this to 'tensions', within the work, between speech and silence, movement and stasis, narrative and anti-narrative (of course all these categories could be deconstructed). To tell the story of civil war is, in a sense, to repeat, and thus to be implicated in, its evil. A key word to describe that evil, within the *Pharsalia*, is *nefas*, the unspeakable; hence 'Lucan hates, spurns, defers, resists his projected narrative.'[27] Epic is a telling of events, and in the *Pharsalia* Caesar is, inevitably, the main actor, the creator and controller of the plot, as he overleaps the moral boundaries in the footsteps of Hannibal and of Alexander the Great (as developed by the rhetoricians, the type of the tyrant and overreacher). By contrast Pompey merely delays, or seeks to delay, the actions of his rival. But, Masters observes, Lucan's work, while it reflects both characters, is, in obvious respects, more like Caesar's, massive, wild, excessive, transgressive, in a word 'Caesarean'. So Nero/Caesar is appropriately Lucan's Muse. The tension is, in a sense, terminal. As Rome and the universe self-implode, so the text collapses in on itself, as its massive structures are massively blocked.

Masters' thesis receives support from the poem's reception. The transgressive Marlowe, attracted by Lucan as by Ovid, produced an energetic translation of *Lucan's First Book*, arguably one of the underrated masterpieces of Elizabethan literature; not implausibly he may have been attracted, partly, by the figure of the overreacher Caesar. Certainly such transgressors – Tamburlaine and Faustus – were a powerful presence within Marlowe's dramatic imagination, and the arguments about whether they are 'true' heroes, supermen who rightly ignore the moral restraints that fetter their pigmy compatriots, and whom we should admire, or whether they stand morally condemned before the world, re-enact the tensions within the *Pharsalia* which Masters describes. Similar arguments rage round the figure of Milton's Satan, who may well also descend, in part, via Marlowe's overreachers, from Lucan's Caesar. The idealization of Caesar is not without relevance for Europe's own civil wars during our century, even if few have been quite as open in their commitments as Macaulay who, in 1835, wrote,

---

[26] Feeney (1991), 285.
[27] Henderson (1988), 134; cf. Feeney (1991), 276–7; Masters (1992), 1–10 and passim.

after rereading the *Pharsalia*: 'The furious partiality of Lucan takes away much of the pleasure which his talents would otherwise afford . . . The manner in which he represents the two parties is not to be reconciled with the laws even of fiction . . . Caesar, the finest gentleman, the most humane conqueror, and the most popular politician that Rome ever produced, is a bloodthirsty ogre.'[28] The road to Mommsen's Caesar and German expansionism is already open. James Welwood, in the introduction to Nicholas Rowe's widely-admired, posthumously-published translation of the *Pharsalia* (1718), probably compiled from the poet's own notes, pays tribute to how much of Caesar's 'true' quality shines through: 'His greatness of mind, his intrepid courage, his indefatigable activity, his magnanimity, his generosity, his consummate knowledge in the art of war, and the power and grace of his eloquence are all set forth in the best light upon every proper occasion.'[29] In short the *Pharsalia* is readily construed as a 'Republican' poem, but it also contains the traces of a pro-Caesarean narrative; hence this tendency, among readers, to treat Caesar as the 'true hero' of the poem, the character with whom Lucan – and we – can secretly empathize. Thus we can construct an author-centered account in which Lucan is an outspoken supporter of the 'Good Old Cause', but we can also modify this with a text-centered, 'reception'-based account in which other meanings become possible. This deconstructive turn is scarcely surprising, since civil war problematizes, in a quite fundamental way, both word and world, by revealing the mobility of the sign normally effaced by appropriation and accommodation, and by the operations of ideology.

We can end with the lacerated body of a 25-year-old poet, the marvellous boy. And the corpse of a truncated poem which ought never to have been written, the poem of the unspeakable, of *nefas*. It breaks off without closure, without *telos*. For there was nowhere to go. And poetry cannot save us; indeed, if we try so to use it, it may corrupt us – and we it. These fragments have I shored against my ruins. Why, this is Hell, nor am I out of it. The rest is silence. *Gott ist ein lauter Nichts* . . .

Retractation?

I have offered these brief readings, *exempli causa*, to show one form a criticism concerned with the historical reception of texts might take, and

---

[28] Quoted in Duff (1928), introduction, xii–xiii.   [29] Cited Martindale (1986), 213.

left aside the more difficult theoretical and epistemological issues involved. One word which has been largely missing from these accounts is 'appropriation'. But, it could be argued, appropriation was always, precisely, the real name of the game, for was I not (for example) appropriating Marlowe appropriating Ovid, and, while so doing, suppressing just those operations of *différance* which, elsewhere, I have freely acknowledged? Or, to put the point in a rather different way, it is hardly surprising if my reading of Marlowe should have affected my reading of Ovid, given that I was applying the same set of (mildly poststructuralist) moves to both texts. One possible response would be that, if there is a bind here, it is one we cannot avoid. Interpretation is not something we can choose to do or not to do; *to read is to interpret*, and to read in one way is inevitably not to read in some other(s). (One could compare Wittgenstein's famous duck-rabbit, which can be seen either as a duck or as a rabbit but not as both *at precisely the same time*.) And to interpret necessarily involves holding something still, however much we might subsequently seek to destabilize it again. Comparisons of (say) Ovid and Marlowe usually presuppose that the two writers constitute fixed points, as it were, which we can observe from a third point 'outside' either. If, on the other hand, the account of reading offered in the first chapter is accepted, it sets both 'Ovid' and 'Marlowe' in motion, and also means that their relationship is always already interlinked in various ways, since 'Marlowe' has been part of the process of the construction of 'Ovid', and *vice versa*, and so on (*ad infinitum*); moreover the reader is herself entrammelled within the discourses which constitute both. *We read from within a tradition, or a discourse, or a set of reading practices, or we do not read at all.* As a result a sharp distinction between the two writers and the interpreter implodes. Any movement in the case of 'Ovid' accordingly involves movement in 'Marlowe', in 'the reader', and so on. Much more simply, if our views of Ovid and Marlowe are constantly changing, then so too must be our comparisons of the two writers.

In practice, few, if any, will seek to deny that there is a significant relationship between (say) Ovid and Marlowe, or Ovid and Titian. The differences are about how the character of that relationship is to be described, or, as I would prefer to put it, (re)constructed and (re)negotiated. And here two of the discursive poles are regularly supplied by those familiar terms, 'similarity' and 'difference', and the value put upon them within any critical discourse. Any Ovidian artist or writer can be represented as 'like' Ovid, or as 'unlike' Ovid – to the extreme point of being 'anti-Ovid' (a claim made for numerous such artists and writers) – and likewise valued for being like, or unlike, or both in shifting combinations. For instance, Donne's elegies are often seen as clever modernizations of Ovid's witty and amoral erotic poetry. But – and this is true with Ovid too – we could always decide not to identify the speaker of the poems with the writer, and this separation would open up a gap for oppositional readings (e.g. satiric or feminist readings), which, for example, would make it more difficult to condemn the elegies for their offensive 'maleness', or lack of morality, or whatever. If this strategy is employed with Donne alone, we soon arrive at an anti-Ovidian Donne ('it is Ovid unmasked and brought to face and do service to the reality of a love that is depicted in its full and mysterious seriousness'[30]). A historical discourse can then be invoked to valorize the distinction; Donne's Christianity can be contrasted with 'the Roman Ovid's merely voluptuary smugness', 'the young man's *Playboy* world' – but can we really get back *behind* Christianity (anyway not one thing) in the way this judgement requires us to do but, in its very terminology, might also be said to deny the possibility of doing? In other words 'Donne' and 'Ovid' remain inextricably complicit with each other, in our sense of either or both, if, that is, we belong to a cultural tradition in which both have been in any way prominent. Similarly for Francis Meres in 1598 Shakespeare was the sweet, witty soul of Ovid restored – whereas most modern critics, whose Ovid and Shakespeare are anyway unlikely to be 'sweet', are more concerned to argue that Shakespeare remoulds, renegotiates, perhaps implicitly criticizes and certainly 'improves upon' Ovid. And to either claim we could, of course, retort: '*Whose* Shakespeare is like/unlike *which* Ovid?' Similarly, within discussions of imitation versus plagiarism, each term requires the other for its operations, but the line between them can never be drawn with any finality – indeed it is precisely this lack of finality which makes the discussion worth having in the first place. The master-term which, beyond any other, we use to negotiate these problems of sameness/difference in our handling of texts is *translation,* and it is to translation and the epistemological problems which it raises, and seeks to circumvent, that we must now, finally (re)turn.

[30] Bedford (1989), 78, 65, 63.

74

Translation as rereading:
Symphony in three movements

'How Do You Like London?' Mr. Podsnap now enquired from his station of host, as if he were administering something in the nature of a powder or potion to the deaf child; 'London, Londres, London?'

The foreign gentleman admired it.

'You find it Very Large?' said Mr. Podsnap, spaciously.

The foreign gentleman found it very large.

'And Very Rich?'

The foreign gentleman found it, without doubt, enormément riche.

'Enormously Rich, We say', returned Mr. Podsnap, in a condescending manner. 'Our English adverbs do Not terminate in Mong, and We Pronounce the "ch", as if there were a "t" before it. We say Ritch.'

'Reetch', remarked the foreign gentleman.

'And Do You Find, Sir', pursued Mr. Podsnap, with dignity, 'Many Evidences that Strike You, of our British Constitution in the Streets Of The World's Metropolis, London, Londres, London?'

The foreign gentleman begged to be pardoned, but he did not altogether understand.

'The Constitution Britannique', Mr. Podsnap explained, as if he were teaching in an infant school. 'We say British, But You Say Britannique, You Know' (forgivingly, as if there were not his fault).

'The Constitution, Sir.'

The foreign gentleman said, 'Mais, yees; I know eem.'

Our Mutual Friend

'Do you known Languages? What's the French for fiddle-de-dee?

    'Fiddle-de-dee's not English', Alice replied gravely.

    'Who ever said it was?' said the Red Queen.

75

Alice thought she saw a way out of the difficulty, this time.
'If you'll tell me what language "fiddle-de-dee" is, I'll tell you the French for it!' she exclaimed triumphantly.
But the Red Queen drew herself up rather stiffly, and said,
'Queens never make bargains.'

Through the Looking Glass

'When I mention religion, I mean the Christian religion, and not only the Christian religion, but the Protestant religion, and not only the Protestant religion but the Church of England.'

Thwackum in *Tom Jones*

1 Allegro ma non troppo: praising metaphrase

This chapter will explore some of the implications of reconceptualizing translation as a key testing ground for hermeneutics. Frequently in the past translation has been accorded a relatively low status, partly because of the firm distinction traditionally made between translation and 'original' writing. However, theories of intertextuality have destabilized this particular distinction: *all* texts are enmeshed in other texts. Increasingly too there has been a recognition of the importance of translation as a central cultural transaction. In the words of Walter Benjamin, 'Translation is so far removed from being the sterile equation of two dead languages that of all literary forms it is the one charged with the special mission of watching over the maturing process of the original language and the birth pangs of its own.'[1] So translation studies have burgeoned as they have become a site for the discussion of meaning and interpretation (hermeneutics, semiotics), speech and communication (linguistics) and cultural transference (anthropology).[2] On this view processes of understanding become modes of translation, and the reader is translated into a translator. As George Steiner puts it, an interpreter is 'a translator between languages, between cultures and between performative conventions.'[3]

We may start the discussion with the taxonomy (metaphrase–paraphrase–imitation) set out by John Dryden in a famous passage from the *Preface to Ovid's Epistles* (1680):

[1] Benjamin (1970), 73; cf. Steiner (1975) *passim*.
[2] So Bassnett-McGuire (1980), introduction and ch. 1.   [3] Steiner (1989), 7.

All translation, I suppose, may be reduced to these three heads:
First, that of metaphrase, or turning an author word by word, and line by line, from one language into another. . . . The second way is that of paraphrase, or translation with latitude, where the author is kept in view by the translator, so as never to be lost, but his words are not so strictly followed as his sense, and that too is admitted to be amplified, but not altered . . . The third way is that of imitation, where the translator (if now he has not lost that name) assumes the liberty not only to vary from the words and sense, but to forsake them both as he sees occasion; and taking only some general hints from the original, to run division on the ground-work, as he pleases . . .

Concerning the first of these methods, our master Horace has given us this caution:

* * * *

Nor word for word too faithfully translate; as the Earl of Roscommon has excellently rendered it. Too faithfully is, indeed, pedantically: 'tis a faith like that which proceeds from superstition, blind and zealous.

Dryden's threefold scheme is premissed, like most other accounts of translation, on the assumption that the meaning of a source text is fixed and largely known (or at least knowable). The question then becomes how best to convey this meaning in the target language. For the time being we may leave that assumption in place, and probe Dryden's arguments a little without shifting, in any fundamental way, the terms of the discourse. We can give this discussion the form of an encomium of metaphrase, conducted from the perspective of the metaphrast, and start by looking at examples of the first two of Dryden's categories (we can ignore imitation, on the grounds that Dryden himself is unsure whether it is really a species of translation at all, and that arguably the main criterion of success is the quality of the English poetry that results, not its relation to the original).[4]

> What slender youth, bedewed with liquid odours,
> Courts thee on roses in some pleasant cave,
>   Pyrrha, for whom bind'st thou
>   In wreaths thy golden hair,

[4] For a fuller version of the argument see Martindale (1984b).

Plain in thy neatness? O how oft shall he
On faith and changed gods complain, and seas
   Rough with black winds and storms
   Unwonted shall admire,

Who now enjoys thee, credulous, all gold,
Who always vacant, always amiable
   Hopes thee, of flattering gales
   Unmindful! Hapless they

To whom thou untried seem'st fair! Me in my vowed
Picture the sacred wall declares t'have hung
   My dank and dropping weeds
   To the stern god of sea.

Quis multa gracilis te puer in rosa
perfusus liquidis urget odoribus
   grato, Pyrrha, sub antro?
     cui flavam religas comam,

simplex munditiis? heu quotiens fidem
mutatosque deos flebit et aspera
   nigris aequora ventis
     emirabitur insolens,

qui nunc te fruitur credulus aurea,
qui semper vacuam, semper amabilem
   sperat, nescius aurae
     fallacis. miseri, quibus

intemptata nites; me tabula sacer
votiva paries indicat uvida
   suspendisse potenti
     vestimenta maris deo.

The encomiast might praise this version, by Milton, of *Odes* 1.5 for attempting to mimic numerous specific features of the original in a way that no 'paraphrase' (in Dryden's sense) could. First, there is the number and the (very approximate) shape of the stanzas, together with the lack of rhyme and the means by which syntax and rhythm can be used to 'compensate' for this lack; these include the unusual handling of enjambment, with complex sentences cutting across stanza divisions. (So Milton reproduces the climactic effect of holding back the phrase *simplex munditiis* to the beginning of the second stanza, thereby creating a considerable release of verbal energy at this point.) Then there is the flexible word order and the emphasis given by it to particular words and phrases. For example, the revelation that Horace has been one of Pyrrha's lovers requires the shock effect of beginning the final sentence with *me*, an abrupt transition recreated by Milton. It may take the Latinless reader a few moments to work out that the man is 'credulous', the woman 'all gold', but the inversions of the next two lines, though convoluted, pose no such problems. There are obvious limits here to what is possible as a result of the differences between Latin and English syntax, and the fact that Latin is more fully inflected, thereby allowing a greater freedom in word order. One would hardly translate the first line as 'What many slender you boy among a rose', since the syntactic relations, indicated in Horace's intricately interwoven texture by the case endings, would be wholly obscure. (Horace's word order may be mimetic: the *gracilis puer* surrounds the girl (*te*), as the roses in turn surround the lovers.) Again, the praiser of metaphrase might continue, something of the original's concentration is represented, for example by the avoidance of the definite and indefinite article (of which there are only two instances), as in 'the stern god *of sea*'. Milton is also careful not to dilute the controlling sea image with the addition of further imagery, and retains as much as he can of the alien verbal texturing (for example, 'liquid odours'). In all these ways, the encomiast could argue, Milton catches the otherness, the alterity of Horace's lyric manner, rather than producing a typical seventeenth-century lyric. Certainly Milton's version is astonishingly innovatory, both linguistically and rhythmically, in terms of more normal contemporary practice. Interestingly, in this connection, no one knows for certain when Milton composed it; the suggestions range from 1626, before the 'Nativity Ode', to 1655, by which time the poet had almost certainly begun work on *Paradise Lost*. This uncertainty is the more remarkable in view of the changes in Milton's style over these years. Milton, as it were, empties himself, in 'humility', before the genius of another, and the result is a kind of apparent 'timelessness' (a point to which we shall return).

The praiser of metaphrase could contrast Milton's Pyrrha with an admired example of paraphrase by Dryden himself, his version of the 'Soracte Ode' (1.9):

> Behold yon' mountain's hoary height
>   Made higher with new mounts of snow;
> Again behold the winter's weight
>   Oppress the lab'ring woods below;
> And streams with icy fetters bound
> Benumbed and crampt to solid ground.
>
> With well-heaped logs dissolve the cold,
>   And feed the genial hearth with fires;
> Produce the wine that makes us bold
>   And sprightly wit and love inspires;
> For what hereafter shall betide –
> God, if 'tis worth His care, provide.
>
> Let Him alone with what He made,
>   To toss and turn the world below;
> At His command the storms invade;
>   The winds by His commission blow,
> Till, with a nod, He bids them cease,
> And then the calm returns and all is peace.
>
> Tomorrow and her works defy,
>   Lay hold upon the present hour,
> And snatch the pleasures passing by,
>   To put them out of fortune's power;
> Nor love nor love's delights disdain –
> Whate're thou get'st today is gain.
>
> Secure those golden early joys
>   That youth unsoured with sorrow bears,
> Ere withering time the taste destroys
>   With sickness and unwieldy years!
> For active sports, for pleasing rest,
> This is the time to be possessed;
> The best is but in season best.

The pointed hour of promised bliss,
 The pleasing whisper in the dark,
The half-unwilling willing kiss,
 The laugh that guides thee to the mark,
When the kind nymph would coyness feign,
And hides but to be found again.
These, these are joys the gods for youth ordain.

Vides ut alta stet nive candidum
Soracte nec iam sustineant onus
 silvae laborantes geluque
  flumina constiterint acuto.

dissolve frigus ligna super foco
large reponens atque benignius
 deprome quadrimum Sabina,
  o Thaliarche, merum diota;

permitte divis cetera qui, simul
stravere ventos aequore fervido
 deproeliantes, nec cupressi
  nec veteres agitantur orni.

quid sit futurum cras fuge quaerere, et
quem fors dierum cumque dabit lucro
 appone, nec dulces amores
  sperne puer neque tu choreas,

donec virenti canities abest
morosa. nunc et campus et areae
 lenesque sub noctem susurri
  composita repetantur hora,

nunc et latentis proditor intimo
gratus puellae risus ab angulo
 pignusque dereptum lacertis
  aut digito male pertinaci.

While she might applaud Dryden's rendering as an English poem, the praiser of metaphrase could claim that it misses the 'tone' of the original and its 'sense' (notice that on this view tone is something we 'read off' rather than 'read in'). Tone, she could argue, is built up from a vast number of tiny details and, by changing many of these details, Dryden necessarily changes the tone. Words, that is, (particularly in poetry) are not just a dress to clothe the meaning, they are the meaning: change the words and you change the sense ('letter' and 'spirit' are in that sense inseparable) – the best translation is therefore the one which changes least. Dryden's firm, confident rhythms may create an attractive conviviality, but the metre is too crisp, too jaunty, with too much of a snap, to convey Horace's more stately motion. Likewise Dryden's version is too long-winded, and overly argumentative; the mood is too breezy for Horace's measured and oblique recommendation of present enjoyment. In his 'Restoration' way Dryden is more openly preoccupied with sex (though Horace's interest in Thaliarchus *could* have an erotic dimension). There is nothing about wine inspiring love in Horace's second stanza, and no kissing in his last, just a laugh in a corner and a forfeit snatched from a young woman's arm. The offbeat and under-stated ending is spoiled by Dryden, who also irons out the syntactic complexities on which Steele Commager has written: 'Four modifiers without substantives initiate us into the confusion; the arrangement of words is as intricate and as puzzling as the event itself. Our very effort to overcome the difficulty of the lines involves us in them, and the text becomes a context of reality.'[5] In lines 11–18 Dryden introduces overtly Christian overtones and a Christian sense of the providential nature of the universe. There is a delight, more Ovidian perhaps than Horatian, in the violence of the weather (as an index of God's power) and in the majesty of creation; in Horace the operations of the gods are more mysterious, and there may be a hint of death in the mention of the cypresses. Stanza 4, in Dryden's rendering, again misses Horace's measured hedonism: Dryden's firmly-expressed instructions (cf. the urgent male chauvinism of 'these these' in his final line), in contrast with Horace's negative commands, are overly definite, febrile, and hedonistic. Horace's dances disappear, to be replaced by 'love's delights'. Magnificent verse though it is, Dryden's fifth stanza removes the metaphor which, it could be said, helps to control and unify Horace's diverse

[5] Commager (1962), 53–4.

pictures and his *paraenesis*. Critics have often noted, and some have complained, that a poem which begins in winter near Mount Soracte ends in Rome in spring in the Campus Martius. This is achieved by a series of deft transitions (where Dryden is notably less deft), but the poem holds together because of an implicit association of whiteness, winter, snow, old age and death on the one hand and greenness, spring, youth and love on the other. The antithesis is made explicit in stanza 5 by the juxtaposition of *virenti* and *canities*, the latter looking back to the *candidum* of line 1 (we might render 'while gloomy whiteness is absent from you in your green youth'). Now indeed, the praiser of metaphrase could conclude, we might even prefer Dryden's version, *as a poem*, to the original, for its vigorous expression of male sexual desire, but that is a different matter from calling it a satisfactory translation.

At this point our encomiast (if of a certain theoretical sophistication) might attack the 1680 Preface on a wider front. If Dryden's threefold scheme is based simply on the degree of 'literalness', then the various cut-off points become arbitrary, and in practice most translations will fluctuate in this regard. We might prefer to think of translations as falling at various points along a line from extreme freedom at one end to exact metaphrase at the other. If, however, the distinction between metaphrase and imitation is a different one whereby (as it were) the latter brings the poem to the reader and the former reader to the poem, that is, is not merely a question of the degree of freedom but points to a different underlying *principle*, then it is hard to see in what sense paraphrase could legitimately be regarded as occupying middle ground between two such different principles. Indeed she could argue that the scheme is not so much arbitrary as tendentious: Dryden wishes to create the impression that paraphrase is the virtuous Aristotelian mean between the vicious extremes of freedom and metaphrase. There is something underhand too in invoking the authority of Horace, who, in the *Ars poetica*, is not talking about translation in the narrower sense at all, but about the writing of 'original' Latin poetry on the model of the Greeks, about *imitatio*. In general a danger with paraphrase is that it makes translations produced in a given period sound alike, and, as a result, the alien quality of the originals is not respected, the reader's sensibilities are not substantially stretched and the target language is not enriched. By contrast, the practitioner of metaphrase, who is alert to this homogenizing danger, seeks not to soften the idiosyncrasies and mannerisms which help to make an author's style distinctive, but to highlight them. For example, he will retain rhetorical figures, like metonymy, rather than substitute more 'normal', non-figurative language (e.g. by translating *Volcanus* as 'fire'). And indeed such figures can be accommodated in English, as when Shakespeare, in Prospero's renunciation speech, writes 'Ye elves of hills, brooks, standing lakes and groves; | And ye that on the sands with printless foot | Do chase *the ebbing Neptune*' (*Tempest* v.i.33–5). On occasion he will simply transliterate: Christians today would find it inconvenient to manage without the Hebrew words 'Amen' and 'Alleluia'. Transliterations like this – and also calques, for example the Latin *unigenitus* for Greek *monogenēs* – are one of the ways a language enriches itself. The metaphrast will avoid resolving perceived ambiguities in the original (for instance, about whose tears are meant, Aeneas' or Anna's or Dido's, in *Aeneid* 4.449 *lacrimae volvuntur inanes*), or neutralizing extended linguistic usages – thus he will prefer to render *Aeneid* 4.67, *tacitum vivit sub pectore vulnus*, as (say) 'the silent wound lives beneath her breast' rather than (say) 'the wound remains concealed beneath her breast'. In this way that original remains partly 'other', clearly belonging to a different culture, not assimilated into the new one to the point of invisibility. It is not surprising that a number of modernists – intent on forms of 'defamiliarization' – have chosen this metaphrastic path (Pound's *Homage to Sextus Propertius*, for example, contains many metaphrases). On this view, in short, it is clear what answer Alice should have given the Red Queen: the French for 'fiddle-de-dee' is – 'fiddle-de-dee'.

It would not, of course, be difficult for Dryden, or another supporter of 'paraphrase', to find rejoinders to these arguments. For example, he could claim that Milton's 'Pyrrha' ignores the resources of the English language to its own detriment, and also that its appeal is likely to be limited to those who already know the original Latin. It lacks the elegance which paradoxically goes with Horace's density, and misses the tone (amiable malice?). A more far-reaching objection would be that the view of language implied in such an encomium of metaphrase is atomistic and lexical. The lexical equivalence of words (e.g. *amor* = love) is taken as the key to this mode of translation, although such linguistic equivalence is a very different matter from 'sameness' (thus *amor* does not always 'mean' what an English-speaker means by 'love'). Words, as any structuralist would tell us, are part of a structured system of contrasts, and meaning is anyway always situational and contextual. Translation is thus a problem in semiotics, not in word-for-word lexical equivalence. It would be merely perverse to translate 'quel age avez-vous?' by anything other than 'how old are you?' (or the like). A metaphrastic rendering of such a phrase – or of (say) a proverb – would only produce unidiomatic nonsense; in cases like these we must translate 'sense for sense'. And so the argument might continue. However, I leave any further stages in this particular argument for the reader to pursue for herself, and instead wish to swerve, in order to destabilize Dryden's scheme, and the discussion it has engendered, in a rather more radical way.

2 Adagio maestoso: untying the text

This is the point in the chapter which in a sonnet would be called the *volta* or 'turn', the point at which we begin to untie the text. And here we may introduce a new 'voice', that of Borges in his fable 'Pierre Menard, Translator of the Quixote', which explores some of the paradoxes inherent in the idea of translation.[6] Menard, out of a desire for '*total* identification' with his author, labours to translate *Quixote* into Cervantes' 'original' words: 'his admirable intention was to produce a few pages which would coincide – word for word and line for line – with those of Miguel de Cervantes'. The result, however, is still not similitude: the two texts 'are verbally identical, but the second is almost infinitely richer . . . The contrast in style is also vivid. The archaic style of Menard . . . suffers from a certain affectation. Not so that of his forerunner, who handles with ease the current Spanish of his time.' Thus the 'same' words *mean differently*:

> It is a revelation to compare Menard's *Don Quixote* with Cervantes's. The latter, for example, wrote (part one, chapter nine):
>
> > . . . truth, whose mother is history, rival of time, depository of deeds, witness of the past, exemplar and adviser to the present, and the future's counsellor.

---

[6] Borges (1970), 62–71; the quotations are from pages 65, 66, 69, 68. The irony, impossible to quantify, is radically destabilizing: but if Menard's project is taken either with entirely po-faced seriousness or as merely mad, the story might have little point.

Written in the seventeenth century, written by the 'lay genius'
Cervantes, this enumeration is a mere rhetorical praise of history.
Menard, on the other, writes:

> . . . truth, whose mother is history, rival of time, depository
> of deeds, witness of the past, exemplar and adviser to to the
> present, and the future's counsellor.

History, the *mother* of truth: the idea is astounding. Menard, a
contemporary of William James, does not define history as an
enquiry into reality but as its origin. Historical truth, for him, is
not what has happened; it is what we judge to have happened.
The final phrases . . . are brazenly pragmatic.

As I have already observed, discussions of translation usually assume
that the meaning of the original is fixed, and that the translator's task is to
reproduce it as far as possible in the target language; any argument is
about the appropriate mode for so doing. But if meaning is not so fixed
but constantly reconstructed, contextually and discursively, by communities of readers, then no translation, even an interlinear 'construing', is
ever 'innocent', but always an act of interpretation, of rendering
readable, which might involve (for example) foregrounding some
elements and erasing others. If, as in the final quotation from Borges, the
same words have different meanings in different contexts and within
different reading practices (in this case one attuned to historical change
and the 'author function'), how could identity of meaning ever be
achieved in a translation? Translation, like interpretation, becomes
rather a saying in other words, a constant renegotiation of sameness-
within-difference and difference-within-sameness. Those seeking the
'correct' translation are thwarted by linguistic difference and history ever
on the move. Of Menard's project Borges writes 'It is not in vain that
three hundred years have gone by, filled with exceedingly complex events.
Among them, to mention only one, is the *Quixote* itself.' Furthermore
writing a translation always has hidden implications, in the very act of
choosing what to translate, about the nature of literature and the status
of the original. A good translation is commonly supposed to convey the
poetic quality of that original, but the notion of what constitutes good
writing is itself always on the move.

As a result of this, a Gadamerian formulation, that in translation one
is learning to say in one's own words what one finds in the words of

someone else,[7] can be represented both as a truism and as an occlusion of the complex mechanisms by which this process operates. Of course there are conventions of lexical equivalence, but even a simple word like *panis* has a quite different semantic range from 'bread',[8] and that range is itself not something fixed but subject to change. The nature of that equivalence will accordingly vary, not only between different periods, but between different speakers within the same period; there is, however, sufficient overlap for 'communication', *in some form*, to take place. The lack of exact fit between different languages and within different languages means, as has already been noticed, that in language-use equivalence is not equivalent to sameness. Where the gap between equivalence and sameness is most strongly felt, we talk of *untranslatability*. Thus a scholar who has no qualms about translating *panis* as 'bread', or *et* as 'and', may falter when it comes to *virtus* or *pietas*, and may prefer to transliterate (itself of course a form of translation) rather than substitute an already existing English word. In some cases the ideological significance of a choice of equivalence is, or eventually becomes, easy to perceive. For example *hamartia* in Aristotle's *Poetics*, previously often translated as 'moral flaw', is now more frequently rendered 'mistake' or the like. It was not simple ignorance of Greek that led to the now discarded rendering; nor has the change occurred because of fresh lexical evidence. The (mis)interpretation of *hamartia* was, it can be argued, fuelled by latent Christian assumptions; if so it was ideological and not (merely) lexical factors which shifted the perspective from which Aristotle's text was interpreted. But that does not mean that 'our' translations are simply 'right', 'natural', or unperspectived, or any less appropriative and dependent on prior assumptions and paradigms than those of previous generations (Aristotle's function within 'our' culture and the view of what his writings are 'for' have shifted). For example, the translation 'sacred' or 'holy' for *sanctus*, rather than (say) 'sanctioned', could be said, in our culture, to be Christianized already. Frequently the relevant considerations are partly social or political. A colleague once remarked to me that no one would translate *arma virumque* by 'arms and the bloke'. But a language community could arise (indeed may already have arisen) in which this would be a viable translation, and the observation, one could feel, tells us as much about social attitudes in contemporary Britain as it does about 'Virgil's' phrase: questions of decorum and of linguistic sociology are not so easily separable.

[7] So Warnke (1987), 110–11.   [8] Cf. Bassnett-McGuire (1980), 18–19.

MacIntyre, who usefully links the notions of translation and tradition, illustrates 'untranslatability' with an instance of an ideologically highly charged case of naming:

> Consider as an example the two rival place names 'Doire Columcille' in Irish and 'Londonderry' in English. 'Doire Columcille' embodies the intention of a particular and historically continuous Irish and Catholic community to name a place which has had a continuous identity ever since it became St Columba's oak grave in 564 . . . while 'Londonderry' embodies the intention of a particular and historically continuous English-speaking and Protestant community to name a settlement made in the seventeenth century, information about whose commercial origin in London, England, is conveyed as effectively by its name as the corresponding information is conveyed by 'Doire Columcille'. To use either name is to deny the legitimacy of the other. Consequently there is no way to translate 'Doire Columcille' into English, except by using 'Doire Columcille' and appending an explanation. 'Londonderry' does not translate 'Doire Columcille'; nor does 'St Columba's oak grave', for in English there is no such name.[9]

This is part of MacIntyre's attempt to present a model of translation in the light of untranslatability. When a person learns a new language, she starts by learning supposed equivalents, and then, as she becomes more inward with the new language, she learns what is untranslatable. The problem here resides in the sharp division betweeen translatability and untranslatability. For what is true in MacIntyre's strong case of a contestation of names would be true in other weaker cases. Thus *Roma* would not translate adequately as 'Rome' because the linguistic differences, with their various traces, within the two signifiers are not identical. Indeed, as we have seen, no two users of the 'same' language use names, or words in general, identically, since the field of meaning will vary in each case. Learning to operate effectively in a foreign language does not freeze *différance*, any more than does learning one's first language and inhabiting it comfortably. Each time we use words we affirm, or contest, or (re)negotiate, their meaning, in the new context. This mobility of linguistic signs, the presence within them of more meaning than can ever

[9] MacIntyre (1988), 378.

be grasped by any particular user, and the various strategies of accommodation, of appropriation, which result from this, mean that language is and is not translatable, always and never.

On this view Dryden's threefold scheme does not have to be abandoned, but it does have to be reconceptualized. We could say that the original text becomes not a fixed but a moving target, and so more difficult to hit (indeed, as we shall see, this particular metaphor breaks down). And something analogous is true of the other points in the triangle of text–translation–reader. Literary theorists have unfixed, destabilized each of these points, in the (re)turn from positivistic to anti-foundationalist models of interpretation, even if in practice something has to be held still for detailed discussion of a text to take place at all. The difference between translation and interpretation is dissolved, and translation is seen not as reproducing but as (re)constructing the 'original' (whose fully originary status is thereby denied), determining the ways in which it is read. Dryden's three modes then become different ways of conceiving *how texts mean*. The argument is no longer about which mode best represents the original, but about what implications for meaning are inscribed in each mode. Metaphrase, even if it could be represented as depending on a theoretically vulnerable conception of lexical equivalence at the level of the individual word, tends to result in a process of making strange. By contrast paraphrase and imitation tend to elide any gap between past and present, and thus to stress continuity and similarity. Difference and similarity are here viewed as discursive constructions. It is always possible to represent an ancient poem as 'like' or as 'unlike' later poems. Translation, in short, negotiates the discursive space generated within the poles of 'similarity' and 'difference', in a way which is always and never arbitrary. A choice of mode is always also susceptible of a political or ideological interpretation. Humanistic defences of paraphrase and imitation could be linked to a desire to establish continuities between antiquity and the modern world in the interests of conformity. By contrast Milton's preference for metaphrase, which drives a wedge between 'then' and 'now', could be seen as part of his political iconoclasm.[10]

Within this discourse the distinction between 'literal' and 'free' translations (like the often-made distinction between 'letter' and 'spirit' contested earlier by the encomiast of metaphrase), and with it the

---

[10] For some different, but analogous speculations see Potter (1989), 51–7.

conceptualization of the three modes in terms of degrees of literalness or fidelity, comes under pressure. 'Faithful to what?' we have to ask; 'whose literalness? which fidelity?' Bentley supposedly once remarked to Pope, of his version of the *Iliad*, that 'it is a pretty poem, Mr Pope, but you must not call it Homer.' But that is to raise the question, precisely, of what Homer 'is'. We could reply, on Pope's behalf, that he had found a collectively equivalent though different set of linguistic terms, concepts and relations to represent the Homeric world, within the language available to him, and that his frequent echoes of post-Homeric poems like *Paradise Lost* and Dryden's *Aeneid* were justified on the grounds that these works had helped to determine what Homer had come to 'mean', that there is no access to Homer outside the epic tradition within which his poems have been inscribed. For a historicist like Bentley Pope's *Iliad* was not Homer, but for a reception theorist the situation is very different. Pope's *Iliad* itself, together with its reception both admiring and hostile (including, of course, Bentley's critique) is part, and not an unimportant part, of the construction of 'Homer'.

Translation thus becomes a sign of change, a sign of what it means to be a human being 'after Babel', and also a sign 'that no one language is adequate'.[11] And we have to learn to live with that inadequacy. Walter Benjamin retains, by contrast, a desire to return to Eden.[12] He finds, behind the act of translation, a search for 'that ultimate essence, pure language', a language 'which no longer means or expresses anything but it, as expressionless and creative Word, that which is meant in all languages'. Predictably the closest that we come to it is in the Bible, which is, in Benjamin's view, 'unconditionally translatable' (otherwise how could we all find salvation through it?), and he concludes that 'the interlinear version of the Scriptures is the prototype or ideal of all translation'. Thus a preference for metaphrase (Benjamin's favoured mode) can be represented as having a metaphysical dimension. The argument was advanced earlier that Milton's 'Pyrrha', while from one point of view creating a sense of strangeness, also produces an impression of timelessness, because it does not seem clearly to reflect the norms of language of the time when it was written. Is metaphrase then an attempt to create 'the-text-as-Other-in-itself'? It is anyway unsurprising that Benjamin rejects any stress on reception: 'in the appreciation of a work of

[11] Edwards (1984), 164, 176.
[12] Benjamin (1970), 79–80, 82, 69. Benjamin's views are deconstructed by Derrida (1985); cf. Robinson (1991), 218–49.

art . . . consideration of the receiver never proves fruitful.' The reception theorist, by contrast, may be content to live within the constraints of time and history.

One problem about laying so strong an emphasis on the slippage involved in all language exchanges is that it may seem to deny the possibility of any fruitful dialogue, any understanding of the other, whatever. And our desire for stories seems to be predicated on a desire for otherness. What are the implications of claiming that dialogue – including translation – always involves slippage? Of course there can be an agreement to control slippage (e.g. between an airline pilot and ground control), but such dialogues are, in important respects, unlike our dialogues with poetry. In general the appropriative nature of dialogue serves to oil the works, smoothing routine human intercourse. And some dialogue evidently breaks down, or otherwise fails, as an act of communication. There have been attempts, within pragmatics, to restrict the free-play of meaning within dialogue by an appeal to the notion of 'optimal relevance', a concept associated with Dan Sperber and Deidre Wilson which has recently been applied to translation theory.[13] The principle is a useful one no doubt. If I ask you about your health, and you respond by holding up a medicine bottle, depending on the context I may interpret this – on the assumption that you have correctly heard my question (and are not mad) – as a statement that you are feeling unwell. But even if this interpretation accords with your own understanding of the act, it hardly exhausts the semiotic significance even of this simple exchange (holding up a medicine bottle is pretty evidently different from saying 'I am unwell'). While 'relevance' may well be a tacit criterion within most reading practices (but again whose relevance?), it can hardly be employed to congeal all the results of *différance*, nor, even if it could, would that necessarily be desirable. Dialogue, like love, requires at least two participants; total similitude might reduce two to one, and thereby collapse dialogue. We may think of dialogue, diagrammatically, as the partial overlap, sometimes more, sometimes less, between two or more semiotic fields, or two or more fields of consciousness. It involves a negotiation between differences, many of which may not be clear even to the communicators. Exchange and interchange are evidently possible (though not necessarily achieved as often as we like to believe) in consequence of a mutual appropriation of their positions by the

---

[13] See Gutt (1991) for translation as interpretative relevance across languages.

participants, but do we ever know as we are known? And, if we did, would 'we' any more be 'we'? (a question to which I shall return in the coda to this book).

Some of these issues can be focused by looking at the passage from *Our Mutual Friend* which is cited at the beginning of this chapter.[14] What is involved in understanding across linguistic barriers? In the exchange between Podsnap and the foreign gentleman a failure of communication is made droll. We have a striking instance of irreducible Podsnappery, into which nobody can ever break, because there is no chink for any alternative view. But what of the dialogue between reader and writer which frames it? Is Dickens communicating with us across the gulf between the two characters? In a sense, if the passage amuses and engages us, an affirmative answer is possible. But can we ever be sure what is at issue? For example, suppose we condemn Podsnap as pretentious, vulgar and complacent; are we not, by this act of cost-free self-congratulation, becoming ourselves complacent snobs? Any such reading for the moral runs the risk of degenerating into cliché and positionality. How far are our own conversations – with foreigners, with children, even with our friends – representable as disconcertingly 'like' Podsnap's? How far indeed can we understand the exchange in the novel? Podsnap's central question about the British Constitution is extraordinarily opaque, and it is hard to know (he might not know himself) whether the foreigner is puzzled at a basic lexical level, or rather by the obscure drift of the question. Are we, in other words, just like Podsnap, patronizing the foreigner? The harder we look at the passage, the stranger, the more elusive, it seems; the more there is always a supplement. Can we enact closure in one way only, by an exercise of Podsnappery? And so is 'Dickens' laughing with us, or at us?

3 Allegro vivace: unlocking the word-hoard

 If translation is inseparable from interpretation, and if reading can profitably be seen as a form of translation, enquiry into translation becomes an important part of the hermeneutic process. For example, in chapter 2, I argued for a particular account of the significance of Aeneas' visit to Pallanteum, one based on its conflation of 'pastoral' and 'epic' elements. It is therefore instructive that Dryden's version (like Claude's

[14] I am grateful to Michelle Martindale for ideas on this passage.

painting already analysed) foregrounds this generic fusion in a way which, from some perspectives, might seem like over-translation, but which could help us towards a reading along these lines:

> The fiery sun had finished half his race,
> Looked back, and doubted in the middle space,
> When they from far beheld the rising towers,
> The tops of sheds, and shepherds' lonely bowers,
> Thin as they stood, which then of homely clay
> Now rise in marble from the Roman sway.
> These cots, Evander's kingdom, mean and poor,
> The Trojan saw and turned his ships to shore.
>
> (translation of *Aen.* 8.97–101)

Direct study of translations – including those translations which have been especially influential or which, for a variety of reasons, we may especially admire – ought to assume a greater importance within the pedagogic procedures of Classicists than is usually the case at present. The precise hermeneutic value of such an exercise will obviously be differently conceived according to different conceptions of the relationship between 'original' and 'version'. As we have just seen, on one model a poem has a basically single, stable meaning, which the translator tries to reproduce. On this view a fine translation could help us to arrive at this meaning, but equally we could arrive at it without the translation by a different route. On a modified version of this model translations mobilize different sets of elements in the original to give plausible or possible readings. A good translation selects and arranges, in an effective way, elements which are 'there' in the original, and in doing so may give us a different reading of a poem from the one we previously entertained which we may, on particular grounds, prefer. On an alternative model, involving a more radical untying of the text, translations determine what is counted as being 'there' in the first place, and good translations thus unlock for us compelling (re)readings which we could not get in any other way. 'Tone', for example, becomes, as we have seen, not something read off but something constructed; indeed, within this discourse, the difference between 'reading off' and 'reading in' is dissolved. Our conception of 'Ovid' is mediated through translations like those of Dryden which have helped to define what 'Ovid' is for us. We read in and through translations, though these always imply the possibility of other translations, other readings; indeed comparing a text and a translation necessarily presupposes the presence of a second 'ghostly' translation, which is sometimes called the 'gap' between them (another way of describing the reified text?). We engage in a multi-directional elucidation of texts, in a relationship which may be termed one of 'intertextual mutuality'.[15]

On any of these views one could argue that translation makes a poem readable *as a whole* in a way that commentary alone cannot, or at any rate offers a different kind of whole. So we can now turn, in a fairly pragmatic spirit, to an admired instance of 'paraphrase', Dryden's 'Cinyras and Myrrha', (one chosen by David Hopkins to illustrate his view that Dryden had a special artistic affinity with Ovid[16]), in order to see what heuristic value may reside in reconceptualizing translation as a form of interpretation. The story of Myrrha (*Met.* 10.298–518) is one of a number of stories – others are those of Pygmalion, Byblis and Iphis – which deal with cases of 'deviant' sexuality, although to use the word 'deviant' is, of course, already to have interpreted, since the distinction between the 'normal' and the 'deviant' is one which the stories might be said to challenge or deconstruct. The standard modern books on Ovid have surprisingly little to say about these stories – except that of Pygmalion which is usually taken as a fable about art and life – partly perhaps because of embarrassment about their subject matter (sex and Latin scholarship often make uneasy bedfellows). By contrast writers and artists throughout the centuries have repeatedly been drawn to Myrrha's tale at least. Ovid's status as a canonical writer legitimated treatment of what might otherwise have been forbidden, unspeakable matters.

For Brooks Otis stories like Myrrha's evince variations of the same basic pattern: 'a perverted *libido* is wholly unable to secure its object and, as a result, becomes isolated and dehumanized.' Myrrha herself 'is the extreme instance of human degradation to a sub-human form', and her metamorphosis, treated as the appropriate consummation of her choice, is, he declares, 'a kind of death, a real loss of human consciousness and identity'.[17] (Other scholars avoid taking a position on how far Myrrha deserves her end, an end which could rather be seen as liminal between human life and death.) It is striking how analogous is Otis' account to the schematic allegorizations found in many medieval and Renaissance

[15] I owe this approach to Tom Mason; cf. Robinson (1991), ch. 2.

[16] Hopkins (1985) and cf. (1988). I also learned much from a seminar conducted by David Hopkins on this topic.   [17] Otis (1970), 269, 228–9.

94

commentaries. Ovid's story is read, in traditional allegorical terms, *moraliter* and *in malo*, as a negative *exemplum*; and there is a similar tendency to become obsessed with reified abstractions like *libido*. On such a reading gloom and sadness, not unsurprisingly, prevail, as they do in Arthur Golding's version in his complete translation of 1567, where Myrrha's desire for her father becomes a 'filthy love', 'wickedness', 'sin'. By contrast others read the story as a Euripidean psychological melodrama, sympathetic to women and their feelings, but undercut by a certain amount of frivolity, as in the opening warning to readers about the horrible character of the story (300–3) which L.P. Wilkinson, for example, characterizes as 'jaunty'.[18] One alternative would be to see these lines as in character for the teller Orpheus, either in his role as religious mystagogue (*procul hinc natae, procul este parentes*, 300, 'be far away from these mysteries, daughters and fathers'), or in his role as poet (since the passage could be said to raise questions about the status of belief, of fictions, of poetic authority, and about the relationship between an artist and his reception). Dryden, it may be observed, has, to some extent, recontextualized the story by publishing it as a separate piece, rather than as one of a number of stories told by Orpheus; as a result there is less sense of a dissemination of authority among different authors than there is in the original with its Chinese-box-like structure.

Dryden's version can be used to suggest a rather different, more complex, interpretation of the story than Otis', to which Myrrha's opening monologue (319–55) provides the key, a passage which Dryden gives thus:

> Ah, Myrrha, whither would thy wishes tend?
> Ye gods, ye sacred laws, my soul defend
> From such a crime as all mankind detest,
> And never lodged before in human breast!
> But is it sin? Or makes my mind alone
> The imagined sin? For nature makes it none.
> What tyrant then these envious laws began,
> Made not for any other beast but man?
> The father-bull his daughter may bestride;
> The horse may make his mother-mare a bride.
> What piety forbids the lusty ram,
> Or more salacious goat, to rut their dam?

[18] Wilkinson (1955), 207.

The hen is free to wed the chick she bore,
And makes a husband whom she hatched before.
All creatures else are of a happier kind,
Whom nor ill-natured laws from pleasure bind,
Nor thoughts of sin disturb their peace of mind.
But man a slave of his own making lives,
The fool denies himself what nature gives;
Too busy senates, with an over-care
To make us better than our kind can bear,
Have dashed a spice of envy in the laws,
And, straining up too high, have spoiled the cause.
Yet some wise nations break their cruel chains,
And own no laws but those which love ordains,
Where happy daughters with their sires are joined,
And piety is doubly paid in kind.
O that I had been born in such a clime,
Not here, where 'tis the country makes the crime!
But whither would my impious fancy stray?
Hence hopes, and ye forbidden thoughts, away!
His worth deserves to kindle my desires.
But with the love that daughters bear to sires.
Then had not Cinyras my father been,
What hindered Myrrha's hopes to be his queen?
But the perverseness of my fate is such,
That he's not mine, because he's mine too much.
Our kindred-blood debars a better tie,
He might be nearer, were he not so nigh.
Eyes and their objects never must unite,
Some distance is required to help the sight.
Fain would I travel to some foreign shore,
Never to see my native country more:
So might I to myself myself restore,
So might my mind these impious thoughts remove,
And ceasing to behold, might cease to love.
But stay I must, to feed my famished sight,
To talk, to kiss – and more, if more I might.
More, impious maid! What more canst thou design?
To make a monstrous mixture in thy line,
And break all statutes, human and divine?

Canst thou be called (to save thy wretched life)
Thy mother's rival and thy father's wife?
Confound so many sacred names in one,
Thy brother's mother! sister to thy son!
And fear'st thou not to see the infernal bands,
Their heads with snakes, with torches armed their hands,
Full at thy face the avenging brands to bear,
And shake the serpents from their hissing hair?
But thou in time the increasing ill control,
Nor first debauch the body by the soul;
Secure the sacred quiet of thy mind,
And keep the sanctions nature has designed;
Suppose I should attempt, the attempt were vain;
No thoughts like mine his sinless soul profane,
Observant of the right; and o, that he
Could cure my madness, or be mad like me!

'quo mente feror? quid molior?' inquit,
'di, precor, et pietas sacrataque iura parentum,
hoc prohibete nefas scelerique resistite nostro –
si tamen hoc scelus est. sed enim damnare negatur
hanc Venerem pietas: coeunt animalia nullo
cetera dilectu, nec habetur turpe iuvencae
ferre patrem tergo, fit equo sua filia coniunx,
quasque creavit init pecudes caper, ipsaque cuius
semine concepta est ex illo concipit ales.
felices, quibus ista licent! humana malignas
cura dedit leges, et quod natura remittit
invida iura negant. gentes tamen esse feruntur
in quibus et nato genetrix et nata parenti
iungitur, ut pietas geminato crescat amore.
me miseram, quod non nasci mihi contigit illic,
fortunaque loci laedor! – quid in ista revolvor?
spes interdictae, discedite! dignus amari
ille, sed ut pater, est. ergo, si filia magni
non essem Cinyrae, Cinyrae concumbere possem.
nunc quia iam meus est, non est meus, ipsaque damno
est mihi proximitas, aliena potentior essem?
ire libet procul hinc patriaeque relinquere fines,

dum scelus effugiam; retinet malus ardor amantem,
ut praesens spectem Cinyram tangamque loquarque
osculaque admoveam – si nil conceditur ultra.
ultra autem spectare aliquid potes, impia virgo?
et quot confundas et iura et nomina sentis!
tune eris et matris paelex et adultera patris?
tune soror nati genetrixque vocabere fratris?
nec metues atro crinitas angue sorores,
quas facibus saevis oculos atque ora petentes
noxia corda vident? at tu, dum corpore non es
passa nefas, animo ne concipe neve potentis
concubitu vetito naturae pollue foedus!
velle puta; res ipsa vetat. pius ille memorque
moris – et o vellem similis furor esset in illo!'

Dryden, Hopkins argues, sees as central to the story the question of Natural Law, its complexities and contradictions. The discourse of nature (sometimes opposed to, sometimes conjoined with law) is explored to the point where tensions and fissures begin to emerge, and awkward questions are raised. In other words the *differences* within the term 'nature' are exposed, with a resulting slide, disconcerting or distasteful to some, invigorating to others. Thus the 'serious' categories through which the Romans appear to have conceptualized their world and articulated their values are subjected to a scintillating deconstructive play. One of the most basic of these category distinctions is that between human beings and animals, and the passage explores the significance of these categories within accounts of our sexuality. Are the ways we think of family and sexual relationships eternal truths, or rather the result of local conditions and conventions? If it is 'natural' for animals to mate with their offspring, why is it not also natural for human beings to so? Is it 'natural' for men and women to act 'unnaturally'?[19] Is 'morality' relevant only to human beings, and is it then 'natural' or 'unnatural'? In describing animal couplings Ovid's Myrrha wittily uses vocabulary more often (naturally?) associated with human intercourse (*fit equo sua filia coniunx*, 326, 'his own daughter becomes the horse's spouse'), so that the

---

[19] So Feeney (1991), 195–7. For other scholarly readings closer to 'mine' or 'Dryden's' see Ahl (1985), 213; Barkan, (1986) 70–1. It should thus be clear that my point is not that Dryden is preferable to modern critics simply because he is 'right' and they are 'wrong'.

language itself dissolves what elsewhere are key boundary-markers. On this account the story alerts us to the possible relative nature of the moral terms we use (in opposition to their more fixed and hegemonic use in 'respectable' Augustan discourse). *Pietas*, for example, is a central term in Virgil's *Aeneid*; with Myrrha we find a paradoxical *pietas*, a love pushed (too?) far beyond its (proper? natural?) limits.

In his prose writings Dryden was sometimes critical of what, in the Preface to *Fables*, he termed Ovid's 'boyisms', the stylistic 'turns' (tropes) and arabesques which have so often troubled sober readers of the *Metamorphoses*. But his version, or so Hopkins argues, speaks rather of a delight in such 'excesses'. One effect of the self-conscious play of language is to remind us that, on one level, Ovid is the author of the speech, and controls the speaker like a skilful puppet-master. The ostentatious verbal finesse with which Myrrha presents the argument about animal sex is, in conventional terms, 'out of character', 'unwomanly' ('unnatural'?); one might recall, by way of contrast, Dido's desire to live like a wild thing (*Aen.* 4.550–1, *non licuit thalami expertem sine crimine vitam | degere, more ferae*, 'I wasn't allowed to live my life, like an animal, without crime, free from marriage'), which would generally be regarded as stylistically appropriate to her character and mood, and which Ovid perhaps glances at here (for further possible Virgilian echoes see e.g. 300, 307–9, 369–70, 375). Such linguistic appropriateness is precisely one mechanism by which ideologies – including the way we view our sexual roles – naturalize themselves, as Ovid's 'boyisms' can remind us, if we allow them to jolt us out of our conventionality. At the beginning of the episode Orpheus contrasts his own country with the exotic East, where luxury and such sexual aberrations as incest flourish (304–10). The contrast is conventional in Roman moral discourse, except that here it is not Rome and Italy but Thrace (normally itself contrasted with Rome) which is set against the Orient. Could it be, we might be led to ask, that we all constitute our own country as the norm, other countries as deviations?

Ovid, as we say, is 'playing with fire'. Such people are apt to get their fingers burnt (or worse). And here I would emphasize the word 'play'. In lines 346–8 Myrrha scrambles (*confundas*) a set of terms usually kept quite separate: 'Will you be called sister of your son and mother of your brother?' In *Oedipus the King* such fearful scrambling will bring Oedipus' world down in ruins. Myrrha will eventually flee her native land and become a tree; and the terror of category confusion can certainly be felt in her metamorphosis, as hard bark encroaches, graspingly, on soft female flesh. But in Myrrha's speech the elegant paradoxes and antitheses and pointing and balancing create an exuberance of language which could, just, take the sting out of moral death. For here we might find – with Dryden as our co-interpreter – an odd sort of delight, a kind of child-like play. Ovid is in Wonderland, where the categories that rule our world can, in imagination at least, be temporally suspended, as the signifiers dance free of their signifieds. That, at any rate, is what I now find 'in' Ovid, and what I first found in Dryden's Ovid – or should it be Ovid's Dryden?

The reader is probably ready for the final deconstructive twist in the argument.[20] If Dryden's Myrrha is an interpretation, then the reader has been interpreting an interpretation of an interpretation. . . . And the series does not end with the-text-as-it-really-is-and-was-and-will-be. The signs – and even these change their shape – have to be read, and every reading, even that (or those) of the author, is, on this view, an act of translation. So we have no final 'text', but rather an ever-widening fan of 'translations', which can always be supplemented by another translation. If translation, as I have been arguing, can usefully be conceptualized, not as a uni-directional process but rather as a dialogic one of intertextual mutuality, we have a situation in which 'texts' which are always already translations speak to other texts, including readers as textually-constituted subjects. Like history, the conversation will never stand still, so long as there are people to participate in it. So it is history and conversation – which is always a conversation in at least two languages[21] – which are the enemies to those seeking fixity. The rest of us may rejoice that the conversation is a continuing one. Texts always mean *more* (which is not the same as saying that they mean whatever one likes), and more can always join in.

---

[20] For this trope I must acknowledge Duncan Kennedy as *il mio miglior fabbro*. It is worth quoting Stephen Hinds's 'unpacking': 'your description of your reading of Dryden–Ovid in terms of signifiers dancing free of their signifieds points to your implication in a powerfully enabling late twentieth-century discourse of post-structuralist criticism, centrally interested in the self-conscious play of language, which helps you to find the Ovid-in-Dryden and Dryden-in-Ovid that you do' (ideology of periodization?).   [21] I owe this formulation to George Myerson.

Postscript: redeeming the text, or a lover's discourse

I fear we are not getting rid of God because we still believe in grammar.
Nietzsche

And God created every living creature that now moveth, and one was man. Mud as man alone could speak. God leaned close as mud as man sat up, looked around, and spoke. Man blinked.

'What is the *purpose* of all this?' he asked politely.

'Everything must have a purpose?' asked God.

'Certainly', said man.

'Then I leave it to you to think of one for all this', said God. And He went away.

The Books of Bokonon (Kurt Vonnegut, *Cat's Cradle*)

Nothing . . . is anywhere simply present or absent. There are only, everywhere, differences and traces of traces.
Derrida

'He was part of my dream, of course – but then I was part of his dream, too!'

Through the Looking Glass

Could we accept Paul de Man's suggestion that 'it is . . . not *a priori* certain that literature is a reliable source of information about anything but its own language'?[1] After all we might wonder quite what 'reliable' means here, or whether, in that case, we could satisfactorily explain why we value some stories over others, or account for the effects they have in

[1] De Man (1986), 11.

our lives (reading books has, not infrequently, led to 'conversions' of various kinds). There would obviously be major ethical ramifications in so extreme a hermeneutic of suspicion. We can here also distinguish the 'sceptic', who, accepting her own contingency and the necessary provisionality of her views, is open, now relaxedly, now passionately, to a wide range of claims and experiences (Montaigne would be a good example) from the 'sceptic', who, either contemptuously or wearily, sees through everything and everyone. A decision to live with *aporia* is a very different matter from abandoning all trust in our fellow human beings; so we may be worried too by the angry Pharisaism which grips a number of 'theorists', in Britain at least, even if it seems so different from the linguistic nihilism of a de Man. Rather they can be represented as the heirs of the Leavisites, whom C.S. Lewis dubbed the 'Vigilant school of critics'. In their case, he wrote, 'criticism is a form of social and ethical hygiene', and they find 'in every turn of expression the symptom of attitudes which it is a matter of life and death to accept or resist'. 'No poem', he observed, 'will give up its secret to a reader who enters it regarding the poet as a potential deceiver, and determined not to be taken in.'[2] Elision of the social and political concomitants, or determinants, of the creation of an aesthetic sphere, could, of course, be imputed to Lewis here, although in practice he was seldom guilty of privileging the purely aesthetic.

Throughout the centuries we can find instances of the trope which represents books, or authors, as our 'friends', and I have already hinted at some of the advantages, and disadvantages, of this way of thinking. Wayne Booth develops the analogy at some length: 'the authors who become our lasting friends are those who offer to teach us, by the sheer activity of considering their gifts, a life larger than any specific doctrine we might accept or reject'; we may conceive a strong desire 'to continue in the company of *this* text to discover what kinds of openness or closure lie ahead', making that 'primary act of *assent* that occurs when we surrender to a story'.[3] Attractive as such a conception as this may be, it has its limitations, not least in downplaying what we might call the 'intransigence' of art. Are Dante and Milton, for example, if we value them, really

---

[2] Lewis (1961), 124–8, 94. Cf. Harrison (1991), 61–70. One could instance the claim that language is a prison, criticized by Weinsheimer (1991), 118 (should we not rather say that language *both is and is not* a prison?).

[3] Booth (1988), 222, 64, 32, and as an instance of a certain 'liberal' complacency e.g. 210.

adequately describable as our 'friends'? Is there not some taming of the text at work here, some refusal to accept the possible *dangers* which can come from 'literature'? But this does not invalidate any comparison of reading and dialogue. In particular the question 'what does this mean?', it has been suggested, can be too 'blankly coercive' a one to ask of any text.[4] According to Gabriel Josipovici, who insists that 'we do not decipher people, we encounter them',[5] reading is best thought of as a 'participation': 'books ask us . . . to *speak* them, not to *know* them . . . We will cease to see books as objects to consult for our salvation or a source of truth or knowledge, and come to see them as beings which ask us to take part in an activity.'[6] This will do quite well, so long as we do not forget that there are some activities in which we might not wish, or might not be able, to participate.

Students of Derrida will not have failed to notice the theological 'traces' in my title. A number of contemporary philosophers – Alastair MacIntyre and Charles Taylor would be two obvious instances – have suggested that many of our intellectual problems arise from the inadequacy (or non-existence) of our enquiries into metaphysical questions. Again and again in this essay I have pointed to the (occluded) metaphysical implications of contemporary scholarship and criticism, which the theoretical turn has helped to bring to light. Language of a type which, in the past two centuries, would have appeared mainly in religious discourse has now been recovered within modern literary theory, in opposition to more dominant logocentric and 'rationalistic' critical modes (though poets have often used an overtly 'religious' vocabulary when discussing poetry). We have heard much from 'radical' critics of the 'political unconscious', but there is also what we can call the 'theological unconscious'.[7] Derridean deconstruction, with its emphasis on 'absence' and the *mise en abîme*, has much in common with negative theology. As Kermode has it, deconstruction 'tries to subvert the myth of presence and offer inexhaustibility as a replacement for plenitude, no rest, honourable or otherwise, for the people of God'.[8] George Steiner talks of the 'wager on transcendence' that occurs whenever we read.[9] Religions offer a possible model for the idea of a tradition, in the sense of a (partly) self-sufficient discourse inhabitable only from within in a (hopefully) non-exclusive communality with others (belief, on this view, is the ability

[4] Leith and Myerson (1989), 151.   [5] Josipovici (1988), 307.
[6] Josipovici (1990), 121.   [7] So Moore (1989), 36, and cf. 148; Hart (1989).
[8] Kermode (1983), prologue, 26.   [9] Steiner (1989), 4.

to inhabit a discourse comfortably). Living as we do amid a babble of words we need, it may be, to be recalled to a sense of the power of the Word, often figured in the Bible as a cutting sword or a consuming fire. Stories can be dangerous things; they make a difference. And Christian theology could provide a possible metaphysical model for certain aspects of the reading process as I have described it. The doctrine of the Trinity, which presents the Eternal Word as always engaged in self-dialogue, mediates between difference and sameness, union and communion. That of Incarnation, by which the Word empties itself of power, to engage in the confusions of history, time and humanness, and to redeem them, could make a plausible allegory of reading. Erasmus replaced the Vulgate's *Verbum* ('word') by *sermo* ('speech', 'discourse'), when he translated the opening of St John's Gospel, 'In the beginning was the Word', thereby emphasizing the rhetorical function of the incarnate Son, the Word made flesh. The idea of Incarnation could be said to mediate between logocentricity, the notion that there is an originary centre for meaning, and non-logocentricity, since speech (*logos*) enters, contingently, the multiform text of the world in stories, causing meaning to be deferred and displaced.[10] And this seems to correspond to a central paradox about interpretation which I have already adumbrated, namely that any text has to be treated *both as transhistorical and as contingent on a particular moment of history* if it is to be interpreted.

Dialogue, as we have seen, is a puzzling phenomenon, even a paradoxical one. How can 'I' both be 'myself' and understand 'you'? Of course we live with such paradoxes much of the time, and not least in the areas of our most cherished 'beliefs'.[11] In his poem 'Jordan I' Herbert argues that poetic rhetoric is of no value for praising God: all the poet need 'plainly' say is 'My God, my King'.

> Who says that fictions only and false hair
> Become a verse? Is there in truth no beauty?
> Is all good structure in a winding stair?
> May no lines pass except they do their duty
>   Not to a true but painted chair?

---

[10] Cf. Moore (1989), 151–70. Is this a point where I began to reify?

[11] Two poems worth pondering upon in this regard are Donne's 'The Ecstasy' and Browning's 'Two in the Campagna'.

Is it no verse except enchanted groves
And sudden arbours shadow coarse-spun lines?
Must purling streams refresh a lover's loves?
Must all be veiled, while he that reads divines,
    Catching the sense at two removes?

Shepherds are honest people – let them sing;
Riddle who list for me and pull for prime;
I envy no man's nightingale or spring;
Nor let them punish me with loss of rhyme
    Who plainly say, 'My God, my King'.

Herbert's argument is self-contradicting, first because to say 'My God, my King' is not to make a poem at all, so that most of 'Jordan I' is *necessarily* wholly taken up with the rhetorical turns it supposedly rejects, and secondly because the final 'plain' affirmation does not escape figurality, since to call God 'King' is to use a metaphor, a figure of speech. By exposing these contradictions the critic 'deconstructs' the poem, producing an *aporia*. She may then notice that a poem which so obviously foregrounds its own rhetoricity could be said to deconstruct itself, and so exhibit the entrapments of language and dramatize its own dilemmas (there is more than a little reification of the text, of course, at work here). Yet, paradoxically, at an emotional level, at the point of reception, the poem achieves, for many of its readers, what it proclaims to be impossible, a move from (apparent) rhetorical intricacy to (apparent) simplicity of affirmation. We may 'see through' even this rhetorical move (is a writer more, or less, honest when he or she draws attention to his or her rhetorical strategies?), but even so we may still be moved. Similarly it is difficult, perhaps impossible, to theorize a reconciliation of power and freedom (each term indeed needs the other), yet in millions of homes some sort of reconciliation is worked out in practice every day. Something worth calling 'communication' is hard to envisage, or describe, but perhaps too – who knows? – may be a fairly commonplace occurrence.

    We might then, I suppose, adopt as a readerly slogan 'love your enemy'. By this I mean that it may be humanly desirable, admittedly against all the odds, to try to be as inward as you can with the positions of the person who disagrees with you, not in some spirit of emulsive compromise, but rather with a full acknowledgement of her radical otherness. Most human exchanges exist in a middle ground of mediation, appropriation, slippage, which has the effect of massaging, or indeed occluding, otherness; we take away from most conversations what we want to take away. Furthermore it may well be the case that some sort of 'conditional essentialism' (i.e. some commitment to a shared 'human nature') is necessary for dialogue to take place (that is, within the discourse there is essentialism for those involved with it), just as there must be some 'conditional *telos*' if conversation is to have any (local) sense of direction. Something worth calling a 'meeting of minds' may in general be a rarer, and more precious, thing than we usually care to acknowledge, and could be seen, precisely, as *a simultaneity of communion and difference.* There are, perhaps, three discourses within which such matters have traditionally been discussed, the discourse of religion, the discourse of eros, and the discourse of art. All three have often been linked, and all three are, not infrequently, dismissed today, with some derision, as 'mystifications', by the radical and the sophisticated.

C.S. Lewis ends *An Experiment in Criticism* with these bold words: 'Literary experience heals the wound, without undermining the privilege, of individuality . . . in reading great literature I become a thousand men and yet remain myself . . . I see with myriad eyes, but it is still I who see. Here, as in worship, in love, in moral action, and in knowing, I transcend myself; and am never more myself than when I do.'[12] Seeing with other eyes – this is certainly a powerful rhetoric; but is Lewis describing an event so paradoxical as to be a kind of miracle? Certainly such a notion of self-transcendence requires that it is played out against a norm of appropriation. We are back again with those paradoxes of sameness-within-difference and difference-within-sameness where we have found ourselves so often before in the course of our discussion. If this paradox can be lived with and reading can be construed as (potentially) dialogic in some such sense as this, then, perhaps, the word is not frozen, not dead, but capable of being redeemed and of redeeming, whenever a reader, accepting her own historicity, makes an act of trust, and commits herself to a text in all its alterity, takes, in other words, the risks – and they would be risks – of being read, of relationship. In such relationships who knows what could be found? Maybe only an absence. But there is always the possibility that, for some reader, somewhere, one day, it will prove to be the Love that moves the sun and the other stars.

12 Lewis (1961), 140–1.

'On the Road Home'

It was when I said,
'There is no such thing as the truth',
That the grapes seemed fatter.
The fox ran out of his hole.

You . . . You said,
'There are many truths,
But they are not parts of a truth.'
Then the tree, at night, began to change,

Smoking through green and smoking blue.
We were two figures in a wood.
We said we stood alone.

It was when I said,
'Words are not forms of a single word.
In the sum of the parts, there are only the parts.
The world must be measured by eye';

It was when you said,
'The idols have seen lots of poverty,
Snakes and gold and lice,
But not the truth';

It was at that time, that the silence was largest
And longest, the night was roundest,
The fragrance of the autumn warmest,
Closest and strongest.

Wallace Stevens

These words of love 'I' have written for . . .

OVER AND OUT

THE MIDDLE

Bibliography

Ahl, Frederick M. (1985) *Metaformations: Soundplay and Wordplay in Ovid and Other Classical Poets*. Ithaca, NY

Auerbach, Erich (1953) *Mimesis: The Representation of Reality in Western Literature*. Princeton, NJ

Bakhtin, M.M. (1981) *The Dialogic Imagination: Four Essays*, trans. C. Emerson and M. Holquist, ed. M. Holquist. Austin and London

Baldwin, T.W. (1944) *William Shakspere's Small Latine and Lesse Greeke*, 2 vols. Urbana

Bann, Stephen (1990) *The Inventions of History: Essays on the Representation of the Past*. Manchester

Barkan, Leonard (1986) *The Gods Made Flesh: Metamorphosis and the Pursuit of Paganism*. New Haven and London

Barolini, Teodolinda (1984) *Dante's Poets: Textuality and Truth in the Comedy*. Princeton, NJ

Barthes, Roland (1973) *Mythologies*, trans. Annette Lavers. London
  (1974) *S/Z*, trans. Richard Miller. London
  (1981) 'The discourse of history', trans. Stephen Bann, *Comparative Criticism* 3: 3–20

Bassnett-McGuire, Susan (1980) *Translation Studies*, New Accents. London and New York

Bedford, R.D. (1989) *Dialogues with Convention: Readings in Renaissance Poetry*. London and New York

Beer, Gillian (1989) *Arguing with the Past: Essays in Narrative from Woolf to Sidney*. London and New York, Introduction 1–11

Benjamin, Walter (1970) 'The task of the translator', in *Illuminations*, trans. H. Zohn, ed. H. Arendt. London. 69–82

Bloom, Harold (1973) *The Anxiety of Influence: A Theory of Poetry*. London, Oxford, New York

Booth, Wayne C. (1988) *The Company We Keep: An Ethics of Fiction*. Berkeley, Los Angeles, London

Borges, Jorge Luis (1970) *Labyrinths*, ed. D.A. Yates and J.E. Irby. Hardmondsworth

Bruns, Gerald L. (1991) 'What is tradition?', *New Literary History* 22: 1–21 (from issue on 'Institutions of Interpretation')

Caesar, Michael (ed.) (1989) *Dante: The Critical Heritage 1314(?) – 1870*. London and New York

Cairns, Francis (1972) *Generic Composition in Greek and Roman Poetry*. Edinburgh

Caputo, John D. (1987) *Radical Hermeneutics: Repetition, Deconstruction, and the Hermeneutic Project*. Bloomington and Indianapolis

Commager, Steele (1962) *The Odes of Horace*. New Haven and London

Culler, Jonathan (1981) *The Pursuit of Signs: Semiotics, Literature, Deconstruction*. London and Henley

    (1983) *On Deconstruction: Theory and Criticism After Structuralism*. London, Melbourne, Henley

Curtius, Ernst Robert (1953) *European Literature and the Latin Middle Ages*, trans. W.R. Trask. London

De Man, Paul (1986) *The Resistance to Theory*. Minneapolis

Derrida, Jacques (1977) 'Signature event context', *Glyph* 1.172–97

    (1980) 'The law of genre', *Glyph* 7.176–229

    (1981a) *Positions*, trans. A. Bass. Chicago

    (1981b) *Dissemination*, trans. Barbara Johnson. Chicago

    (1985) 'Des Tours de Babel', in Joseph F. Graham (ed.), *Difference in Translation*. Ithaca and London. 165–248

Due, Otto Steen (1962) 'An essay on Lucan', *Classica et Mediaevalia* 23.68–132

Duff, J.D. (ed.) (1928) *Lucan*, Loeb trans. London and New York

Eagleton, Terry (1983) *Literary Theory: An Introduction*. Oxford

Edwards, Catharine (1993) *The Politics of Immorality in Ancient Rome*, Cambridge

✗ Edwards, Michael (1984) *Towards a Christian Poetics*. London. Ch. 7 on translation

Eliot, T.S. (1957) *On Poetry and Poets*. London

    (1975) 'Tradition and the individual talent', in F. Kermode (ed.), *Selected Prose of T.S. Eliot*. London. 37–44

Feeney, D.C. (1991) *The Gods in Epic: Poets and Critics of the Classical Tradition*. Oxford

Felperin, Howard (1985) *Beyond Deconstruction. The Uses and Abuses of Literary Theory*. Oxford

    (1990) *The Uses of the Canon: Elizabethan Literature and Contemporary Theory*. Oxford

Fish, Stanley (1980) *Is There a Text in This Class? The Authority of Interpretive Communities*. Cambridge, MA and London

    (1989), *Doing What Comes Naturally: Change, Rhetoric, and the Practice of Theory in Literary and Legal Studies*. Oxford

Fränkel, Hermann (1945) *Ovid: A Poet Between Two Worlds*. Berkeley

Gadamer, Hans–Georg (1975) *Truth and Method*, trans. G. Barden and J. Cumming. London

Galinsky, G. Karl (1975) *Ovid's Metamorphoses: An Introduction to the Basic Aspects*. Oxford

Gillespie, Stuart (1988) *The Poets on the Classics: An Anthology of English Poets'*

Writings on the Classical Poets and Dramatists from Chaucer to the Present.
London and New York

Gorak, Jan (1991) *The Making of the Modern Canon: Genesis and Crisis of a Literary Idea.* London and Atlantic Highlands, NJ

Graff, Gerald (1985–6) 'Interpretation on Tlön: a response to Stanley Fish', *New Literary History* 17.109–17

Greenblatt, Stephen (1988) *Shakespearean Negotiations: The Circulation of Social Energy in Renaissance England.* Oxford

Gutt, Ernst-August (1991) *Translation and Relevance: Cognition and Context.* Oxford

Hardie, Colin (1970) 'Virgil', in N.G.L. Hammond and H.H. Scullard (eds), *Oxford Classical Dictionary*, 2nd edn. Oxford. 1123–8

   (1984) 'Virgil in Dante', in Charles Martindale (ed.), *Virgil and his Influence.* Bristol. 37–69

Harrison, Bernard (1985) 'Deconstructing Derrida', *Comparative Criticism* 7.3–24 (= Harrison (1991), ch. 4)

   (1991) *Inconvenient Fictions: Literature and the Limits of Theory.* New Haven and London

Hart, Kevin (1989) *The Trespass of the Sign: Deconstruction, Theology and Philosophy.* Cambridge

Henderson, John (1988) 'Lucan/the word at war', in A.J. Boyle (ed.), *The Imperial Muse: Ramus Essays on Roman Literature of the Empire to Juvenal through Ovid.* Victoria. 122–64

Hinds, Stephen E. (1987) *The Metamorphosis of Persephone: Ovid and the Self-Conscious Muse.* Cambridge

Holquist, Michael (1990) *Dialogism: Bakhtin and his World*, New Accents. London and New York

Holub, Robert C. (1984) *Reception Theory: A Critical Introduction*, New Accents. London and New York

Hope, Charles (1980) *Titian.* London

Hopkins, David (1985) 'Nature's laws and man's: the story of Cinyras and Myrrha in Ovid and Dryden', *Modern Language Review* 80.786–801

   (1988) 'Dryden and Ovid's "Wit out of Season"', in Martindale (1988), 167–90

Iser, Wolfgang (1978) *The Act of Reading: A Theory of Aesthetic Response.* Baltimore and London

Jameson, Fredric (1981) *The Political Unconscious: Narrative as a Socially Symbolic Act.* Ithaca and London

Jauss, Hans Robert (1982) *Toward an Aesthetic of Reception*, trans. Timothy Bahti, introduction by Paul de Man. Brighton

   (1990) 'The theory of reception: a retrospective of its unrecognized prehistory', in Peter Collier and Helga Geyer-Ryan (eds), *Literary Theory Today.* Cambridge. 53–73

Jenkyns, Richard (1980) *The Victorians and Ancient Greece.* Oxford

   (1989) 'Virgil and Arcadia', *Journal of Roman Studies* 79.26–39

Johnson, W.R. (1987) *Momentary Monsters: Lucan and his Heroes.* Ithaca and London

Josipovici, Gabriel (1988) *The Book of God: A Response to the Bible.* New Haven and London

(1990) 'The Bible in focus', *Journal of the Study of the Old Testament* 48.101–22

Keach, William (1977) *Elizabethan Erotic Narratives: Irony and Pathos in the Ovidian Poetry of Shakespeare, Marlowe and their Contemporaries*. Hassocks

Kellner, Hans (1989) *Language and Historical Representation: Getting the Story Crooked*. Madison

Kennedy, Duncan F. (1993) *The Arts of Love: Five Studies in the Discourse of Roman Love Elegy*. Cambridge

(forthcoming) Review of S.J. Harrison (ed.), *Oxford Readings in Virgil, Hermathena*

Kenney, E.J. (1965) Review of J. Brisset, *Les Idées politiques de Lucain, Classical Review* n.s. 15.297–9

(1986) Introduction and notes to A.D. Melville's translation of Ovid's *Metamorphoses*. Oxford and New York

Kermode, Frank (1967) *The Sense of An Ending: Studies in the Theory of Fiction*. London, Oxford, New York

(1975) *The Classic: T.S. Eliot Memorial Lectures 1973*. London

(1979) *The Genesis of Secrecy: On the Interpretation of Narrative*. Cambridge, MA and London

(1983) *Essays on Fiction 1971–82*. London, Melbourne, Henley

(1988) *History and Value*. Oxford

(1989) *An Appetite for Poetry: Essays in Literary Interpretation*. London

Kuhn, Thomas (1962) *The Structure of Scientific Revolutions*. Chicago

Langdon, Helen (1989) *Claude Lorrain*. London

Leith, Dick and Myerson, George (1989) *The Power of Address: Explorations in Rhetoric*. London and New York

Lentricchia, Frank and McLaughlin, Thomas (1990) *Critical Terms for Literary Study*. Chicago and London

Lerner, Laurence (1988) 'Ovid and the Elizabethans', in Martindale (1988), 121–35

Lewis, C.S. (1961) *An Experiment in Criticism*. Cambridge

Llewellyn, Nigel (1988) 'Illustrating Ovid', in Martindale (1988), 151–66

Lloyd-Jones, Hugh (1990) 'Roman Grand Guignol: Lucan's "Civil War" translated into English verse by P.F. Widdows', *New York Review of Books*, 18 Jan. 39–41

Lyne, R.O.A.M. (1987) *Further Voices in Vergil's Aeneid*. Oxford

MacIntyre, Alastair (1985) *After Virtue: A Study in Moral Theory*, 2nd edn. London

(1988) *Whose Justice? Which Rationality?*. London

(1990) *Three Rival Versions of Moral Enquiry: Encyclopaedia, Genealogy, and Tradition*. London

Macleod, Colin (1983) *Collected Essays*. Oxford

McPeek, James A.S. (1939) *Catullus in Strange and Distant Britain*. Cambridge, MA

Martin, Wallace (1986) *Recent Theories of Narrative*. Ithaca and London

Martindale, Charles (ed.) (1984a) *Virgil and his Influence: Bimillennial Studies*. Bristol

(1984b) 'Unlocking the word-hoard: in praise of metaphrase', *Comparative Criticism* 6.47–72

(1984c) 'Literature and Christian belief', *PN Review* 38. 42–6

(1986) *John Milton and the Transformation of Ancient Epic*. London and Sydney

(ed.) (1988) *Ovid Renewed: Ovidian Influences on Literature and Art from the Middle Ages to the Twentieth Century*. Cambridge

(1992a) 'Redeeming the text: the validity of comparisons of classical and post-classical literature: a view from Britain', *Arion*, 3rd series 1:3. 45–75

(1992b) 'Tradition and modernity' (reflections on Alastair MacIntyre's Gifford Lectures, 1988), *Journal of the Human Sciences*, 5.105–19

Martindale, Charles and Michelle (1990) *Shakespeare and the Uses of Antiquity*. London and New York

Martindale, Charles and Hopkins, David (eds) (1993) *Horace Made New: Horatian Influences on British Writers from the Renaissance to the Twentieth Century*. Cambridge

Masters, Jamie (1992), *Poetry and Civil War in Lucan's Bellum Civile* (Ph.D. thesis, Cambridge 1989). Cambridge

Mayer, R. (ed.) (1981) *Lucan: Civil War VIII*. Warminster

Michaels, Walter Benn (1978) 'Saving the text: reference and belief', *Modern Language Notes* 93. 771–93

Mitter, Partha (1987) 'Can we ever understand alien cultures?', *Comparative Criticism* 9. 3–34

Moore, Stephen D. (1989) *Literary Criticism and the Gospels: The Theoretical Challenge*. New Haven and London

Morson, Gary Saul (1991) 'Bakhtin and the present moment', *The American Scholar* 6. 201–22

Nisbet, R.G.M. and Hubbard, Margaret (1970) *A Commentary on Horace: Odes Book 1*. Oxford

Norris, Christopher (1983) *The Deconstructive Turn: Essays in the Rhetoric of Philosophy*. London

Oakshott, Michael (1933) *Experience and Its Modes*. Cambridge

Otis, Brooks (1970) *Ovid as an Epic Poet*, 2nd edn. Cambridge

Panofsky, Erwin (1969) 'Titian and Ovid', in *Problems in Titian Mostly Iconographic*. London. 139–71

Parry, Adam (1966) 'The two voices of Virgil's *Aeneid*', in Steele Commager (ed.), *Virgil: A Collection of Critical Essays*, 20th Century Views. Englewood Cliffs, NJ. 107–23 (= *Arion* 2 (1963) 66–80)

Patterson, Lee (1987) *Negotiating the Past: The Historical Understanding of Medieval Literature*. Madison

Potter, Lois (1989) *Secret Rites and Secret Writing: Royalist Literature, 1641–1660*. Cambridge

Reeves, Gareth (1989) *T.S. Eliot: A Virgilian Poet*. Houndmills and London

Robinson, Douglas (1991) *The Translator's Turn*. Baltimore and London

Rorty, Richard (1989) *Contingency, Irony and Solidarity*. Cambridge

Rosen, Charles (1990) 'The shock of the old' (Review of N. Kenyon, *Authenticity and Early Music*), *New York Review of Books*, 19 July, 46–52

Sawday, Jonathan (1990) 'The fate of Marsyas: dissecting the Renaissance body', in Lucy Gent and Nigel Llewellyn (eds), *Renaissance Bodies: The Human Figure in English Culture c. 1540–1660*. London. 111–35

Segal, Charles Paul (1969) *Landscape in Ovid's Metamorphoses: A Study in the Transformations of a Literary Symbol*. Wiesbaden

Scholes, Robert (1989) *Protocols of Reading*. New Haven and London

Sinclair, John D. (1971) *The Divine Comedy of Dante Alighieri: Italian Text with Translation and Comment*, 3 vols. London, Oxford, New York

Smith, Barbara Herrnstein (1988) *Contingencies of Value: Alternative Perspectives for Critical Theory*. Cambridge, MA

Steiner, George (1975) *After Babel: Aspects of Language and Translation*. Oxford (1989) *Real Presences: Is There Anything In What We Say?* London and Boston

Strickland, Geoffrey (1991) 'In defence of the humanities', *Salisbury Review*, June. 31–7

Taruskin, Richard (1988) 'The pastness of the present and the presence of the past', in Nicholas Kenyon (ed.), *Authenticity and Early Music: A Symposium*. Oxford and New York. 137–207

Taylor, Charles (1989) *Sources of the Self: The Making of the Modern Identity*. Cambridge

Todorov, T. (1984) *M.M. Bakhtin: The Dialogical Principle*, trans. W. Godzich. Manchester

Veyne, Paul (1988a) *Did the Greeks Believe in Their Myths?: An Essay on the Constitutive Imagination*, trans. Paul Wissing. Chicago and London (1988b) *Roman Erotic Elegy: Love, Poetry and the West*, trans. David Pellauer. Chicago and London

Von Hallberg, Robert (ed.) (1984) *Canons*. Chicago and London

Warnke, Georgia (1987) *Gadamer: Hermeneutics, Tradition and Reason*. Cambridge

Weimann, Robert (1984) *Structure and Society in Literary History: Studies in the History and Theory of Historical Criticism*. Baltimore and London

Weinsheimer, Joel (1991) *Philosophical Hermeneutics and Literary Theory*. New Haven and London

Wethey, Harold E. (1975) *The Paintings of Titian III: The Mythological and Historical Paintings*. London

White, Hayden (1978) *Tropics of Discourse: Essays in Cultural Criticism*. Baltimore (1989) '"Figuring the nature of the times deceased": literary theory and historical writing', in Ralph Cohen (ed.), *The Future of Literary Theory*. New York and London. 19–43

Wilkinson, L.P. (1955) *Ovid Recalled*. Cambridge

Williams, Gordon (1983) *Technique and Ideas in the Aeneid*. New Haven and London

Wiseman, T.P. (1985) *Catullus and His World: A Reappraisal*. Cambridge

Wolf, F.A. (1985) *Prolegomena*, trans. Anthony Grafton, Glenn W. Most and James E.G. Zetzel. Princeton, NJ

Worton, Michael and Still, Judith (eds) (1990) *Intertextuality: Theories and Practices*. Manchester and New York

Wyke, Maria (1987) 'Written women: Propertius' *scripta puella*', *Journal of Roman Studies* 77. 47–61

Index of names

reiteration 16   (→ intervention)

"sanction" - Gad. 17